MW01062334

From
Good Hands
to
Boxing Gloves

The Dark Side of Insurance

Also by David J. Berardinelli

From Good Hands to Boxing Gloves:
How Allstate Changed Casualty Insurance in America
(Trial Guides, 2006, 2008)

From
Good Hands
to
Boxing Gloves

The Dark Side of Insurance

By David J. Berardinelli

TRIAL
GUIDES™

Trial Guides, LLC

Trial Guides, LLC, Portland, Oregon, 97205

© 2008 Trial Guides, LLC

All rights reserved. Published 2008.

Printed in the United States of America.

First printing 2008. Second printing 2009.

ISBN: 978-1-934833-01-8

Library of Congress Control Number: 2008902357

> Trial Guides, LLC
> 2400 SW Park Place
> Portland, OR 97205
> (800) 309-6845
> www.trialguides.com

A different, longer version of this book intended for practicing attorneys was published by Trial Guides, LLC, in 2006 and 2008 under the title *From Good Hands to Boxing Gloves: How Allstate Changed Casualty Insurance in America.*

This book is printed on acid-free paper.

Acknowledgements

There are a great number of people to whom I must dedicate this book. Being so many, time and space unfortunately prevent me from identifying each of you by name. I trust you know who you are. I also trust you know why this book is being dedicated to you, albeit silently—because without your many contributions of knowledge and encouragement this book could never have been written.

First among those few is my dad, Joseph Berardinelli, a biochemical scientist by education and nature. Dad taught me more than how to use logic to solve problems. He also instilled in me, by the example of his own life, a conviction to principle that demands doing the right thing—without regard for whether it might be the less popular or personally damaging thing to do. In the end, his teachings inspired me to take up this fight for the rights of policyholders against the abuses of an insurance industry that has placed its greed for profits above keeping its promises.

Second, I dedicate this book to my clients, José and Olivia Pincheira. José and Olivia represent the hundreds of millions of Americans who for years have faithfully paid ever-rising insurance premiums because they still believe they are buying peace of mind. Unfortunately, José and Olivia also now represent the millions of policyholders who have learned that what they were really paying for were false promises. Without José and Olivia's trust and faith in me and in my pursuit of their case—when so many others would have given up long ago—this book, again, never would have been written.

I must also thank Eugene Anderson, the "dean of policyholder attorneys" in America, for his inspirational example and encouragement.

I owe special thanks to my paralegals Sheila and Renea, who have supported me patiently and loyally through the legal battles that resulted in this book. Special thanks also to my editor, Tina, whose help I greatly needed and whom I appreciate even more greatly. Thanks are also due to Gary, Whitney, Dan, Rebecca, Cindy, Karen, Rob, Charles, Aaron, Andy, Kim, Johnny, Paul, David, Anthony, Ray, John, Art, Pat, and the many others who have lent their knowledge, skills, and encouragement to this endeavor.

Last, but hardly least, I must gratefully acknowledge my wife Deborah, my best friend and biggest fan—who has given the most, too often getting so much less than she deserved in return—during the odyssey that has been my legal career over the past 33 years.

—David Berardinelli
March, 2008

Publisher's Note

This book does not offer legal advice and does not take the place of consultation with an attorney with appropriate expertise and experience.

Attorneys are strongly cautioned to evaluate the information, ideas and opinions set forth in this book in light of their own research, experience, and judgment, to consult applicable rules, regulations, procedures, cases, and statutes (including those issued after the publication date of this book), and to make independent decisions about whether and how to apply such information, ideas, and opinions to a particular case.

Quotations from cases, pleadings, discovery and other sources are for illustrative purposes only and may not be suitable for use in litigation in any particular case.

The publisher disclaims any liability or responsibility for loss or damage resulting from the use of this book or the information, ideas and opinions contained in this book.

ALLSTATE® and "GOOD HANDS"® are registered trademarks of Allstate Insurance and are used in this book for informational purposes only. No affiliation, endorsement, or sponsorship is claimed or suggested.

The internet addresses included as references in this book are accurate as of April, 2008, unless otherwise noted.

Contents

Introduction

W HAT WOULD you do if your house caught fire? After the flames were out, you accounted for your family and pets, and the fire trucks drove away, what would one of your first phone calls be? Chances are, you'd call your insurance company.

This book is about insurance. Specifically, it's about *personal lines casualty insurance,* the kind that we buy for our cars, homes, and possessions. Those of us who study insurance or work in the industry call it *casualty insurance.* Casualty insurance isn't a luxury in today's world—it's a necessity. That's why it's important that casualty insurance be affordable, available, and fair for all Americans.

Insurance industry expert and actuary J. Robert Hunter, Insurance Director for the Consumer Federation of America (CFA), argues that insurance is like a utility.[1] Like electricity or our water supply, insurance is a requirement of modern life. When you buy a house or a car, lenders require insurance. Many state laws require proof of auto insurance in order to drive. Like the telephone or electric power, "it is important to the nation that insurance is broadly and affordably available in the same way as other utilities must be available."[2]

Even though we're required to buy these insurance products, most people know next to nothing about what they're buying. I hope this book will give you some understanding of what you should be getting when you buy a policy, and what you're entitled to expect from the insurance companies who sell them.

For most of my career, I've been a practicing trial attorney.[3] I represent policyholders—the people like you who buy insurance. I have never represented an insurance company. I've spent nearly 30 years suing insurance companies for a living. In addition, I've also spent many years researching the insurance industry and how it's supposed to work. A lot of what I say in this book is based on the knowledge I've gained from years of study and the numerous cases I've tried against insurance companies. I readily admit I'm on the side of policyholders—the people who buy policies. However, I've also attempted to give you accurate and objective information, with references you can check for yourself.

This book specifically discusses Allstate and their claims handling practices. You may think this doesn't apply to you if you're not an Allstate customer. However, what one major insurer does affects all of us. If the house next door to you is damaged and the owners can't afford to rebuild because Allstate won't pay enough, that damaged property affects your neighborhood. If you are in a car accident with someone who has Allstate insurance, you may find yourself receiving inadequate coverage for your injuries or car repairs. Most of all, when one insurer makes a major change in business practices, the other insurers follow suit and make the same changes.

Some information in this book comes from a group of about 12,500 Microsoft PowerPoint slides known in legal and insurance circles as the *McKinsey Slides*. Due to this book and the efforts of many others, you can now see the documents on Allstate's website. For a number of years, I was the only attorney representing policyholders in the country who had seen these documents, *and* was allowed by a judge to publicly disclose what I knew about them.

What I hope you'll see are not just the dots, but how they're connected. These comments are based on my knowledge of the insurance industry and on my exhaustive page-by-page review of these remarkable documents, which you can now see for yourself.

To keep the information in these slides a secret, Allstate tried unsuccessfully to gag me and prevent the publication of my legal book and articles. In fact, until April 4, 2008, Allstate did everything it could to keep this information secret. In some cases, Allstate defied court orders commanding it to produce this information for public inspection.

Despite Allstate's efforts to silence me, I published two legal articles and one legal book about these documents and the practices they describe, two years before Allstate was forced to display them.[4] To my surprise, these legal works began drawing serious attention from the mainstream media. This led to a series of reports about the information you'll read in this book, by media outlets like *BusinessWeek, Money Magazine,* CNN, PBS, *Bloomberg News,* and many others.[5] In these articles, the news outlets reported some incredible statements Allstate made in the McKinsey documents. Among them, that insurance is a "zero-sum game," and that Allstate planned to use "boxing gloves" tactics against its own customers. The public response to these media reports was so strong, I finally decided to rewrite my legal book for the general public.

I want you to know what's going on in the casualty insurance industry. You should know that some insurance companies are taking your money under false promises of full insurance protection for your families, homes, and cars.

I say "false promises" because, as you will see, some insurers have created secret claim systems designed to boost their profits by paying less than the full benefits their policies promise. Unfortunately, more and more insurers are starting to follow in their footsteps. It's hard for an insurer to resist taking more than it should when it sees its competitors not only getting away with the same behavior, but making unbelievable profits as a result.

I hope the information in this book will spread far enough to create a public awareness of the harm that insurers are causing to people. These insurers are more interested in making profits than keeping promises. When informed consumers start refusing to buy from such insurers, the market may force them to abandon the business tactics I describe in this book.

Consumers buy insurance for the *benefits* insurers promise to pay if they have a covered loss. Right now, the only information consumers have to rely on when choosing an insurance company are premium prices, slogans, and TV commercials. None of these tell consumers how to make an informed decision about which insurance company to choose. Lower prices tell consumers nothing about the actual benefits they can expect in return for their premiums dollars. Neither do slogans or TV ads.

I hope this book will inspire consumers to demand that their state legislatures pass strong laws. These laws should require *all* insurers doing business in their state to publish accurate, understandable, and accessible statistics. The statistics should tell consumers how much each insurer is paying in benefits for every premium dollar collected. Then consumers will finally have a chance to see whether the insurance they're buying is worth the premiums they're paying. They'll also be able to see which insurers are keeping their promises, and which insurers are withholding benefits to boost profits.

Now is the time to take casualty insurance out of the shadows of public ignorance and put it into the sunlight of public awareness.

1

The Story Behind the Story

José and Olivia Pincheira

This story starts with two people, José and Olivia Pincheira, who hired me as their attorney.[6] When I first met them, I was struck by how they are living examples of the American dream—hardworking immigrants who made a better life for themselves. Unfortunately, their story with Allstate is also a living example of insurance in America, and it is not a good one.

The Pincheiras emigrated legally from Chile to the United States in 1961, and settled in Santa Fe, New Mexico. Although José had a degree in mechanical engineering from Chile, his English skills weren't so great. For José, finding a job in engineering was out of the question until his English improved. While he worked on his English, José took a job as a night janitor at the local Sears store. At that time, Sears owned Allstate, and Allstate agents worked in Sears stores. José befriended the Allstate agents, Frank Sloan and Dean Yount, who often stayed after closing to finish their work.

José enjoyed practicing his English with Frank and Dean. They were nice to him, despite his limited English skills. José grew to trust and respect Frank and Dean as good and honest people—their relationship would last for decades.

When the opportunity came, José left Sears for a better-paying job. He supplemented his engineering degree with courses from the College of Santa Fe, and improved his English. However, when the couple bought their first car in 1963, José came back to see Frank and Dean, and bought Allstate insurance. When José and Olivia bought their first house, José went to Frank and Dean again to buy insurance from Allstate.

José eventually got a job with the New Mexico State Highway Department, where he worked for 22 years. After he retired from the highway department, he worked another ten years as a consultant for several Santa Fe engineering firms. Olivia's degree was in bilingual education. She worked for over 25 years for the New Mexico Department of Education and retired in 1989. The Pincheiras raised three children, who are now grown with children of their own.

Over the years, José and Olivia bought nearly all their insurance from Allstate. The Pincheiras were loyal Allstate policyholders for almost 35 years. For most of those years, they never needed to make a major claim.

They might still be loyal Allstate policyholders today. However, in 1997, an uninsured drunk driver pushed them off the freeway in a snowstorm, plunging their small pickup down a 20-foot ravine, and left them for dead.

Badly injured, their truck totaled, José and Olivia turned to Allstate for the protection they thought they had purchased with nearly 35 years of premiums and no major claims. Instead of the "Good Hands" treatment they expected, they found themselves battered by boxing gloves.

Allstate denied the Pincheira's claim—essentially forcing the Pincheiras to sue to prove their claim was covered. During the course of that lawsuit, the Allstate agent admitted under oath that she misrepresented information to the Pincheiras.

On October 18, 1999, an Allstate sales agent, Sylvia Encinias, admitted the following. She told José Pincheira that the coverage Allstate recommended (medical payments coverage) was *the same* as uninsured motorist coverage, except for one difference. Uninsured motorist coverage paid for lost wages, and as José and Olivia were retired, they didn't need to replace lost wages. Ms. Encinias said that Allstate had trained her to give this advice, which convinced José and Olivia to buy cheaper insurance. These statements were clearly false, as any competent insurance agent should have known, and meant that José and Olivia did not have the coverage they thought they purchased.[7] However, even after hearing that its agents had misled the Pincheiras, Allstate still sided with its agents.

Under its new "get tough" litigation approach, Allstate forced the Pincheiras to go through a knock-down, full blown trial, even after Allstate knew its agents had misled the Pincheiras. During the trial, Allstate's lawyers accused José of not being truthful, despite the evidence from their own agents. After the trial, the judge sided with the Pincheiras and found their uninsured motorist claim was covered by the policy.

José and Olivia still felt abused and wronged by Allstate's conduct in handling their claim. Allstate had forced them to sue to get their uninsured motorist claims covered, and then paid them essentially nothing for the medical bills under their separate medical coverage. José and Olivia decided to sue Allstate and its agent, David Yount, for misrepresentation and for refusing to pay their medical claims promptly and fairly.

This book tells "the story behind the story," of how and why America's second largest insurance company broke faith with the people who pay the bills—their own customers who buy Allstate insurance.

What is McKinsey?

Sometime before September 1, 1992, Allstate's senior executives approached McKinsey and Company, an international business consulting firm, about doing an "engagement," as McKinsey calls it. That engagement would involve a top-to-bottom redesign of Allstate's entire business—with a special concentration on the way Allstate handles claims. Allstate hired McKinsey in 1992 to undertake this project.

During this engagement, McKinsey teams made numerous presentations on the project to Allstate senior management groups. McKinsey used PowerPoint slide shows to accompany its oral presentations. Allstate distributed a set of slides to each attendee, then collected and saved them after the presentations. Allstate now claims these McKinsey slides are the only remaining documentation of this major redesign project, which took at least eight years.[8]

In 2001, I asked Allstate to produce the McKinsey slides during the Pincheira's case. At the time, there was a lot of speculation among attorneys representing Allstate policyholders around the country about what these slides might reveal. I didn't know what was in them. I never imagined that I would be uncovering what may prove to be some of the most explosive evidence of insurance company misconduct ever discovered.

What I did know was how the claim system McKinsey created for Allstate worked. I already had the publicly available manuals McKinsey created to train Allstate's employees on its new claim system, called Claims Core Process Redesign, or CCPR. I spent many hours reading those manuals. I believed from my years of studying insurance law that McKinsey's claim system was probably based on improper insurance claim goals and tactics. I didn't have any evidence showing *why* McKinsey built CCPR like it did. I still needed proof of McKinsey's real intent and goals in designing Allstate's claims system.

The battle for public disclosure of the story told in the McKinsey slides—a battle that would ultimately transform the Pincheiras' case into one of national significance—began with a request filed on July 16, 2001. The following summary shows the series of events after that request.

Timeline: The McKinsey Slides

Berardinelli Requests McKinsey Slides: July 16, 2001

We requested that Allstate produce the McKinsey slides for the Pincheira's case.

Allstate Refuses to Produce Slides: July–October 2001

Allstate refused to produce the slides in several rounds of back-and-forth with the court.

Judge Orders Allstate to Produce Slides: October 30, 2001

At a hearing in Santa Fe, New Mexico with Judge Art Encinias, Allstate argued that they should not have to produce the McKinsey slides. According to Allstate, the slides contain "trade secrets" which if revealed would "seriously damage Allstate's competitive position."

I argued that Allstate should produce the slides, because much of the information was already publicly available in the CCPR manuals. Allstate had no evidence that its competitors had tried to copy CCPR.

Allstate Asks Judge to Reconsider: November 9, 2001

Allstate filed a motion for reconsideration, asking Judge Encinias to give them another hearing to present additional evidence. Allstate insisted that public knowledge of the McKinsey slides would harm them.

Judge Orders Allstate to Produce Again: November 13, 2001

Judge Encinias signed an order for Allstate to produce the McKinsey slides. This order had no restriction on publicly disclosing the information in the slides.

Allstate Requests Reconsideration: December 7, 2001

At a hearing, Judge Encinias asked Allstate's lawyer to describe the additional evidence Allstate might present, as evidence that the slides should be kept secret. The judge wanted to know how public knowledge of the McKinsey slides would harm Allstate.

Allstate's lawyer said she couldn't give the judge a description, because she "frankly had no idea" what that evidence might be.

Judge Encinias denied Allstate's request for a second hearing.

Judge Encinias again ordered Allstate to produce the McKinsey slides with no restrictions on public disclosure by December 31, 2001.

Allstate Asks Court to Overrule: December 14, 2001

Allstate filed a petition in the New Mexico Court of Appeals, asking the court to overrule Judge Encinias's November 13, 2001 order.

We Ask Judge to Dismiss: December 19, 2001

The Pincheiras filed a motion to dismiss Allstate's petition, because Allstate filed their petition one day late. Allstate should have filed it within 30 days of Judge Encinias's November 13, 2001 order.

Allstate Promises Slides With a Catch: December 27, 2001

Allstate voluntarily offered to produce the McKinsey slides, but with a catch.

Allstate would provide the slides under temporary order preventing their public disclosure, until after the New Mexico Court of Appeals decided Allstate's appeal (filed December 14, 2001).

Judge Encinias granted Allstate's temporary order. Allstate would provide the slides, we would not disclose them unless Allstate lost its appeal. This temporary order would expire if Allstate lost its appeal.

Judge Encinias verified: were his terms "acceptable" to Allstate?

Allstate's lawyer replied that the terms were "very acceptable."

Allstate Delivers Slides: January 15, 2002

Allstate delivered over 12,000 McKinsey documents, filed by date, in four boxes. Most of these were PowerPoint slides.

These slides had a protective watermark printed on them. This watermark made them difficult to read and impossible to scan, photocopy, or enlarge.

Berardinelli Summarizes Slides: January 2002–January 2004

I read and summarized the McKinsey slides, eventually producing a 300-page summary.

Court Dismisses Allstate's Appeal: January 31, 2004

It took the New Mexico Court of Appeals two years to do the math that Allstate filed its appeal one day too late.

The New Mexico Court of Appeals dismissed Allstate's appeal (filed December 14, 2001) to overrule Judge Encinias's order to produce the slides.

The New Mexico Court of Appeals upheld Judge Encinias's order (of November 13, 2001).

Under the deal Allstate made with Judge Encinias on December 27, 2001, we would have the right to disclose the information in the slides 14 days after Allstate's appeal became final, which would be February 14, 2004.

Berardinelli Returns Slides for a New Copy: March 22, 2004

I had the slides, and I could now make them available to the public. However, the actual slides Allstate delivered were useless to me as evidence at trial. Because of the protective watermark, I could not scan, copy, or enlarge them.

I returned my copy of the slides to Allstate, requesting a clean copy. I relied on the deal Allstate made with Judge Encinias on December 27, 2001.

Allstate Refuses to Produce: March 19 and April 17, 2004:
Allstate refused to give us a clean copy of the slides, and refused to return the watermarked copy.

Judge Orders Allstate to Return Slides: June 4, 2004
Judge Michael Vigil (who replaced the retired Judge Art Encinias) ordered Allstate to return the slides.

Allstate refused.

Judge Finds Allstate in Contempt of Court: July 15, 2004
Judge Vigil found Allstate in contempt of court and entered a default judgment for disobedience.

Berardinelli Publishes First Legal Article: August, 2005
I published an article in *The New Mexico Trial Lawyer* with verbatim quotes from the McKinsey slides, taken from my summary notes.[9]

Allstate Asks Court to Stop Publishing: November 15, 2005
Allstate went to court again. They asked the judge to prohibit me from publishing anything else about the McKinsey slides. They also accused me of lying about returning the slides.

Filed Slide Summary as Public Record: December 7, 2005
I filed my 300-page summary of the McKinsey slides as a public record in the Pincheira's case.

Allstate Requests Seal on Court File: December 12, 2005
Allstate filed an emergency motion to seal the court's file on the Pincheira's case because it now contained my summary.

Allstate swore under oath that my summary accurately revealed the information in the McKinsey slides.

Judge Denies Seal: January 23 and February 22, 2006
The judge denied Allstate's emergency motion, clearing the way for me to publish information about the McKinsey slides.

Allstate's Efforts to Protect the Slides

This journey took several years, thousands of attorney hours, and enough trial pleadings to fill 25 volumes in the district court's file. However, this allowed me to tell the McKinsey story publicly. Allstate's legal maneuvering proves how eager Allstate was to prevent this information from becoming public. They were willing to wait for years, tie up our court systems, and spend an inordinate amount of money in legal fees—all to keep this quiet.

Since the publication of my legal book and articles describing the McKinsey slides, Allstate went to extraordinary lengths to keep this information out of the public's hands. In many other cases around the country, Allstate's strategy was to make every plaintiff start from square one. Rather than allow other attorneys to share this information, Allstate insisted that they request the McKinsey slides from Allstate, and then go through years of legal battles to get them. If plaintiffs did get the slides, they could not share them. It appears that Allstate has been ordered at least six or seven times to produce the slides without restriction on public dissemination.[10] Until April, 2008, Allstate refused to obey all of these orders. Instead, Allstate either settled the case by buying off the plaintiff quickly, or strung the case out for years with motions and appeals until the plaintiffs and their attorneys finally gave up.

In one case, a Missouri court entered a contempt order against Allstate on September 12, 2007, for refusing to produce the McKinsey documents. The Missouri contempt order also includes a fine of $25,000 a day until Allstate complies with the order and produces the documents. Until April 4, 2008, Allstate refused to obey the order, despite a fine that exceeded $3,250,000.

On January 16, 2008, the Florida Insurance Commissioner suspended Allstate's license to issue new car insurance policies in Florida because Allstate refused to produce the McKinsey documents.[11] In a news release that day, the Commissioner said: "If Allstate is willing to pay $25,000 per day in fines to a Missouri court for its ongoing failure to provide similar documents, it's obvious to me that it will take more than a monetary sanction to get them to comply with our subpoenas."[12]

Is the McKinsey story in this book worth the thousands of hours it took to bring it to the public? Are the McKinsey slides really so important that publicly disclosing them would seriously harm Allstate's business?

On the other hand, did Allstate taking such unprecedented steps, like defying court orders and subpoenas, because the McKinsey slides show Allstate has made boosting profits more important than keeping its promises to policyholders and the insuring public?

You be the judge.

2

The McKinsey
Business Credo

Greed is Good

> The point is, ladies and gentlemen, that greed—for
> lack of a better word—is good. Greed is right.
> Greed works. Greed clarifies, cuts through, and
> captures the essence of the evolutionary spirit.
> Greed in all of its forms—greed for life, for money,
> for love, for knowledge—has marked the upward
> surge of mankind.
>
> —Gordon Gekko, *Wall Street* (1987)

MICHAEL DOUGLAS won an Oscar™ for his portrayal of
the anti-hero Gordon Gekko in the film *Wall Street*. Gekko's
famous *Wall Street* speech captures perfectly the essence of corporate America's business philosophy—and not just during the late
1980s.

Ironically, thousands of smart, ambitious corporate leaders
from the world's most prestigious business schools have come to
regard the Gekko character as the hero of the movie, not the vil-

lain.[13] For them, Gekko validates a hardball approach to business tactics and the relentless pursuit of ever-higher corporate profits.

While the Gekko character was fictional, the business philosophy he described in *Wall Street* is not. It still thrives in the heart of corporate America, due in large part to the influence of one corporate advisor. It's the same corporate advisor that employs the best and the brightest graduates from those top business schools. That corporate advisor—and the principal cheerleader for the business philosophy described in Gekko's famous speech—is McKinsey & Company.

McKinsey has been called "the high priest of high-level consulting, with the most formidable intellectual firepower, the classiest client portfolio, and the greatest global reach of any adviser to management in the world."[14] By its own account, McKinsey serves as the principal business strategist for 147 of the world's 200 largest corporations.[15]

McKinsey's clients also pay handsomely for its advice. In 2002, McKinsey's top clients were paying $10 million a year, and upwards, for its services.[16] In 2001, McKinsey's largest client—which it refused to publicly name—paid fees to McKinsey of about $60 million a year.[17] It's almost certain those fees have gone up since 2001.

In the early 1990s, McKinsey preached its "greed is good" message loud and often in insurance management circles. McKinsey also preached the virtues of its star client—and then Wall Street darling—Enron Corporation. McKinsey knew a lot about Enron and its business model. McKinsey created it. In fact, McKinsey was Enron's principal advisor and strategist for over ten years before its collapse.

McKinsey's preaching, and the fantastic results its "greed is good" business model was producing at the time for Enron, may have convinced Allstate's top executives to adopt McKinsey's business model. That was a great decision for Allstate's shareholders and those executives.[18] It would prove to be a disaster for Allstate's policyholders and the public.

In a February 2007 article entitled "The Desire to Acquire," conservative commentator Robert Ringer stated: "Though the audience was set up to hiss and boo when Gordon Gekko . . . spewed out those now-famous words 'Greed is good,' the fact is he was absolutely right."[19] Ringer qualified his statement by insisting that greed is good only as long as "you don't use force or fraud to acquire what you desire."

The sad truth, however, is that once a company adopts the "greed is good" business philosophy, profits can never be enough. When greed is good, there is no such thing as too much profit. When Gordon Gekko was asked how much profit was "enough," his response was brutal. "It's not a question of enough, pal. It's a zero-sum game. Somebody wins—somebody loses."

As you will later learn, a zero-sum game is exactly how McKinsey described CCPR to Allstate's top executives. McKinsey told Allstate that CCPR would be designed to treat paying claims like a "zero-sum economic game. Allstate gains—others must lose."[20] McKinsey was really saying that CCPR would be based on its "greed is good" business model.

How an Insurance Company Works

Before we continue, however, you need to know some basic information about how the business of casualty insurance works.

Insurance Premiums—Who Decides What We Pay?

You need to learn how casualty insurance premiums are calculated—including why they go up and when they should go down.

Every premium dollar you pay is divided into three parts:

- Loss costs (about 70¢).

- Overhead and expenses (about 25¢).

- Profit (about 5¢).[21]

The percentage of each premium dollar an insurer pays out in claims is what the industry calls *loss costs*. Loss costs are supposed to represent the amount of money the insurer expects to pay out in claims under all policies issued during a given year.

Loss costs are also the foundation of all casualty insurance premiums. When loss costs go up, premiums also go up. When loss costs go down, premiums should also go down. Casualty premiums also include the insurer's overhead expenses and its profits.

On top of the profits already included in premiums, an insurer gets to keep the investment income generated by those premium dollars while they're still in the insurer's hands.

These are generalizations, of course. Loss costs might be calculated 68.5¢ or 72.6¢ per dollar depending on the insurer's actual experience. Expenses might be calculated 35¢ per dollar. And profit might be calculated at only 3¢ per dollar. These are the premium averages generally accepted by the industry itself, so these are the figures I will use in this book as well.

When an insurer pays out significantly less for claims than the 70¢ per dollar it charges, over a long period of time such as ten years, then its premiums should go down. If the insurer doesn't reduce its premiums under these circumstances, it can be accused of charging excessive rates. Under these same circumstances, there should also be no reason for any insurer to *raise* its premiums and *reduce* the coverage its policies provide. Yet, as you'll see later, this is exactly what Allstate has been doing since 1996.

How Does an Insurer Make Money?

Next, you need some basic information about how a casualty insurance company makes money. An insurer makes money in two ways.

- First, there's the money left over after collecting the premiums, paying the claims, and paying its expenses. That's called *net operating income*.

- Second, a casualty insurer makes money from investing its assets. The assets an insurer invests include the premiums it collects during that policy year and what's called the company's *surplus*. Surplus is the accumulation of all the company's past profits and investments. Money an insurer makes from investing its assets is called *investment income*.

CCPR in Action

Back to our story of Allstate insurance, one need look no further than Allstate's response to Hurricane Katrina. We can see how McKinsey's business plan, enacted at Allstate in the CCPR claim system, works in the real world. More than two years after Katrina devastated large parts of Louisiana, Mississippi and the Gulf Coast, thousands of legitimate Allstate claims remain unpaid or were substantially underpaid. Litigation over homeowner claims is paralyzing the civil justice system on the Gulf Coast.

On August 31, 2005, just days after Katrina hit the Gulf region, Allstate's Home Office sent a memo to its National Catastrophe Team laying out carefully scripted press responses to media inquiries. Allstate wanted everyone to know that "[W]e have a good story to tell."[22] Since it implemented CCPR in 1995 and 1996, Allstate has always had a good story to tell—especially to its shareholders enjoying record returns on their investments.

This resulting "catastrophe within a catastrophe" Allstate caused with claim denials is the direct result of McKinsey's CCPR business plan. The plan is working exactly as McKinsey and Allstate intended. Many insureds settled for the first low offer out of desperation or despair. Some waited for a better offer that never came and then gave up. The rest learned how quickly Allstate's "Good Hands" could turn into boxing gloves if they refused to give in and take pennies on the dollar for their legitimate claims.

As a result, thousands of Allstate policyholders have left the Gulf Coast. They couldn't afford to rebuild on what Allstate was offering, and they didn't have the resources to fight Allstate in court to get fair payment.

As Paul Harvey likes to say, this book tells "... the rest of the story." It lets the public behind the scenes to learn how McKinsey and Allstate planned a "radical" change in the way casualty insurance companies do business. It's a story told using some of McKinsey's own words. It's the story of how Allstate can post record profits year after year while it leaves countless policyholders to face serious financial problems. Allstate created those problems because it didn't fully pay for the losses the premiums were calculated to cover.

Where will this story lead? How much profit will finally be enough for Allstate and its shareholders?

3

Traditional
Insurance Rules

T HE INSURANCE contract creates a unique relationship, unlike those in ordinary contracts. Insurance companies promise trust, peace of mind, and security from loss. However, they don't have to keep their promise until there's an accidental loss covered by the policy.

When an unexpected loss occurs, the insured person has to do without something as important as a car or a home until the insurance company gets around to paying. Not having a car to drive or a home to live in can put you in a serious financial bind. Where are you going to live if your home is damaged or destroyed? How can you afford to pay your mortgage if you have to rent another place to live in? How are you going to get to work to earn money if you don't have a car? Will you lose your job because you can't get to work?

At a time of loss, policyholders are at their most vulnerable. Policyholders need to get paid as quickly as possible so they can get on with their lives. That's why we buy insurance: to come to the rescue when we're facing the kind of financial problems an unexpected loss can create.

On the other hand, the insurance company not only writes the contract; it also acts as the sole judge of who gets paid, when, and how much. This gives the insurer a tremendous advantage over its policyholder when a loss occurs and the policyholder is suffering from financial problems. There's a strong temptation for the insurer to take advantage of the policyholder.

Traditional insurance laws recognize this temptation. Because the insurer controls the money the policyholder needs to recover from the loss, the insurer can delay payment to force the policyholder into accepting a smaller settlement than he or she is entitled to. Traditional insurance laws were adopted to "even the playing field." These rules have evolved over the last 100 years. They are intended to prevent insurers from taking advantage of their superior bargaining position over the policyholder.

Traditional insurance rules require insurers to give equal consideration to the policyholder's interests. That means insurers can't handle claims in a way that makes boosting profits more important than the policyholders' right to full payment. When insurers handle claims the way the traditional rules require them to, the system works like it should. Policyholders with legitimate claims get their benefits paid promptly and fairly. They get fair and honest treatment from their insurers.

The traditional insurance rules are based on two principles, the *indemnity principle,* and the *fiduciary principle.* Taken together, they even the playing field between insurer and policyholder. They enable the insurer to make a legitimate profit while still allowing policyholders to get what they paid for: prompt and fair payment for covered losses.

The Indemnity Principle

Casualty insurance is a unique insurance product. It's different from other kinds of insurance like life insurance. Life insurance pays a set benefit when you die regardless of the cause or consequences of your death.

Casualty insurance is *indemnity* coverage. It doesn't pay a set benefit. It pays as much as the policyholder needs, up to the policy's limit, "to restore an insured to the same financial position after the loss that he or she was in prior to the loss."[23] In the language of insurance, to *indemnify* someone means to make them whole again. That means the insured doesn't get paid more than the actual loss. It also means the insured shouldn't get paid less than what it takes to make the insured whole again. The insurer's duty to pay the *full* amount the insured needs to be put back in the same position he or she was in before the loss is the *indemnity principle*.

An insurer violates the indemnity principle by paying less than the full value of the loss. That doesn't make the insured whole. It leaves the insured worse off financially. You pay the insurance company to assume the financial burden of the loss. If you still have to pay for the part of loss yourself, you're worse off. Your standard of living goes down because you have to borrow, take from savings, or do without, until you can afford to replace the loss. When that happens, you don't get the benefits you paid for when you bought insurance.

The Fiduciary Principle

The *fiduciary principle* was also developed to balance the relationship between insurer and policyholder. This principle is based on the idea that insurers act like banks. Like banks, insurers are entrusted with the public's money (premiums) which they promise to pay out when the public needs it. This idea—that insurers act like banks—has been around for a very long time in insurance law. As the United States Supreme Court stated in 1914:

> The contracts of insurance may be said to be inter-dependent. They cannot be regarded singly, or iso-latedly, and *the effect of their relation is to create a fund of assurance and credit, the companies becoming the depositories of the money of the insured,* possessing great power thereby, and charged with great responsibility…On the other hand, to the insured, insurance is an asset, a basis of credit…It is, therefore, essentially different from ordinary commercial transactions, and…is of the greatest public concern.[24]

Like banks, insurers accept their policyholders' money and keep it for them, promising to pay the full amount of their policy-holders' covered losses. Promising to keep somebody else's money until they need it demands a high standard of conduct on the part of the person holding the money.

A person or entity that holds money or property for the benefit of others is called a *trustee*.[25] The trustee holds property or money belonging to someone else "but does not have the right to benefit personally" from that property or money.[26]

Banks can't tell you it's too much trouble for them to honor your withdrawal slip, or ask you to withdraw less than you need. In the same way, insurance companies shouldn't intentionally delay your claim or ask you to accept less than your claim is worth.

As we've already seen, about 70¢ of every premium dollar is for loss costs. It's the money we give an insurer to keep in order to fully pay our claims. It's our money. It's not the insurer's money. Think of it like a joint bank account with all the policyholders' names on it. We can call this money the *claims account*.

Making a claim is the same as withdrawing money from a joint bank account. That account has your name and thousands of other account owners' names. You can't withdraw all the money in the account, because not all the money belongs to you. You have to prove to the teller who you are and that your name is on the account. That's like providing the insurer with proof that you're covered under the policy for a loss you have suffered.

Since it's a joint account, the teller needs to have some proof of how much in the account belongs to you. The teller has responsibilities to the other account owners (policyholders) to make sure you don't withdraw more than your fair share. However, it's still *your* account. The bank also has a duty to make sure you're able to withdraw all the money you need to put yourself back in the same financial position as before the loss—no more but no less either. In addition, the bank has the duty to do this as promptly as possible.

The bank accepted the responsibility—and the fees—for administering this joint account. Therefore, the bank owes it to you, as one of the owners of the account, to be helpful and assist you in accessing your money. The bank can't make withdrawing your money harder than it needs to be. The bank can't delay paying your money, or force you to jump through needless hoops, in hopes that you'll give up or take less than your fair share of the account. The bank also can't create withdrawal procedures that force account holders to sue the bank as the only way to get their full share from the account.

Most important, the bank can't treat the money in this joint account as its own. The joint account holders own the money, not the bank. The bank can invest or loan the money while it's in the account—that's how the bank makes money. However, the bank can't just dip into this joint account whenever it wants to boost its profits, or pay its shareholders extra dividends, or pay its executives large bonuses. That would be like embezzling from the account owners.

That is how the fiduciary principle works. An insurance company acts like a bank. Like a bank offering a savings plan for college or retirement, the insurer calculates and collects enough money (also called loss costs) each year from *all* its policyholders to hold in a joint claims account. The few policyholders who suffer covered losses during the year can be put back to where they were before the loss. Like a bank, the insurer also charges the policyholders expenses and profit for its services. Together, the loss costs, expenses and profit make up our insurance premiums.

Like a bank, the money the insurer holds in the joint claims account belongs to the policyholders—not the insurer. The insurer holds the money in the claims account for the benefit of its policyholders who will need it for their covered losses. In this sense, the insurer acts like a trustee (or bank) holding someone else's money.

The insurer can invest the money while it's in the account, to make money for itself. However, the insurer can't dip into the claims account whenever it wants to boost its profits, pay its shareholders extra dividends, or pay its executives large bonuses. That would be like taking money for itself that belongs to its policyholders.

Like a bank, the insurer must be helpful and assist its policyholders to withdraw their fair share from the claims account as promptly as possible. The insurer can't deliberately make it harder than it needs to be for policyholders to get the full amount they need to put them back to where they were before the loss.

The insurer can't deliberately delay paying legitimate claims by asking for useless information or demanding more proof than it really needs. It can't delay payment or force policyholders to jump through needless hoops, in hopes they'll give up or take less than the full and fair amount of the benefits they're owed under the policy.

The insurer can't pressure policyholders who are in a financial bind into accepting a quick payment that's far less than what they need to make them whole. It can't deliberately force policyholders to file needless, expensive, and time consuming lawsuits as the only way to get what they need to fully restore them to where they were before the loss.

Together, the indemnity principle and the fiduciary principle encompass the traditional insurance laws and rules that govern how insurers are supposed to treat their policyholders. They also govern how the casualty insurance industry is supposed to operate. Under these traditional rules, insurers owe special duties to policyholders to pay their legitimate claims fairly (the indemnity principle) *and* promptly (the fiduciary principle).

When insurers follow the traditional rules, the insurance system works the way it was intended to work. Policyholders receive fair and prompt payment. Insurance companies earn legitimate profits that keep them solvent and provide a reasonable return to their shareholders.

As a lot of people from around the country will tell you, that's not the way our insurance system is working today. The traditional rules just aren't being followed anymore.

Let's look at how these insurance rules have changed.

4

Insurance and the
Can of Mother's Peas

O NE WAY to better understand the story in the McKinsey slides is to think of buying insurance like buying a can of peas. When you go to the store to buy canned peas, you don't actually see what you're getting. What you see is the label on the can. On the label, it says "Mother's Peas," emblazoned over a picture of ripe peas, beaded with appealing drops of morning dew.

The picture on the label is there to tell you that you're buying peas of the highest quality. That is what you expect to find when you get home and open the can. However, that's not all the label tells you. It also tells you there are ten ounces of peas in the can, and the price is one dollar. You still can't see inside the can. When you go to the check-out stand, you buy your can of peas on faith— faith in the promises the Mother's Peas Company makes on the label of every can of Mother's Peas.

That's what you do when you buy insurance. You can't see what's inside the policy until after you've paid for it. You don't even see the policy itself—with those most important details about what's covered and what's excluded—until after you've paid the premium and the sale is complete.

29

Like that can of peas, you buy insurance on faith—faith in promises such as "You're in Good Hands"™ (Allstate), "Like a Good Neighbor"™ (State Farm), or "We Put You Back Where You Belong"™ (Farmers).

The insurer's advertising slogan is like the picture on the can of peas. It assures you that the unseen promises of protection, like your unseen peas, are worth buying. These insurance slogans are really selling trust in a promise that this policy will provide peace of mind and security from loss. You need to preserve your family's standard of living if a loss occurs, and this promise assures you that this policy will do that.

The premium you pay for insurance is like the price on your can of peas. The coverage limits you've purchased are like the label's promise that there are ten ounces of peas in the can. The coverage limits are a promise that you'll get a full ten ounces of benefits from your can of insurance if you ever need it for a covered loss.

The Half-empty Can

What if, when you open your can of peas, you find it contains only seven ounces of peas instead of ten? You might think the shortage was just a malfunction at the pea-packing factory. You don't like paying a dollar for only 70¢ worth of peas. You want your money's worth. You want a full can of peas. So, you go back to the store and exchange that can for a new one.

What would you think if you found that *all* the cans of Mother's Peas at your local store contained only seven ounces? You'd want to know how and why this happened. You might want to ask some more questions.

What if you discovered a secret set of construction plans for the Mother's Peas factory, proving that the company designed the machines to under-fill *every* can of peas by 30%? What if you also had proof that the Mother's Peas Company did this to generate windfall profits for their shareholders and huge bonuses for their executives? Then you'd probably think you were the victim of fraud.

To complete this analogy, we need to go back to the premium dollar. As we've already seen in "How an Insurance Company Works" on page 17, the insurer is supposed to hold about 70¢ out of every insurance premium dollar in a joint claims account that belongs to the policyholders. That 70¢ is like the promise on the can of Mother's Peas that says there are ten ounces inside. Consumers don't want to pay for *more* peas than the can actually contains. Policyholders don't want to pay for more insurance coverage than the insurer will actually provide.

Policyholders expect Allstate's claim factory to fulfill the promises made on every can of its insurance products. Your most important expectation is the security of knowing your covered losses will be paid fairly and promptly, without being forced to jump through needless adversarial hoops.[27]

You don't expect the manufacturer to design its can of insurance so that you have to use an industrial laser torch to open it. You don't expect to have to hire a professional to open the can for you. You expect to open your can of insurance with little difficulty or delay. Otherwise, the peace of mind promised on the label doesn't mean much.

When your covered losses aren't paid promptly, or are underpaid, it's the same as being charged for a ten-ounce can of peas that contains only seven ounces. You didn't get what you paid for. This is exactly what has happened since McKinsey installed its "greed is good" claim handling model at Allstate.

Payment History at Allstate

Between 1987 and 1996, the casualty insurance industry as a whole paid out an average of 70¢ out of every premium dollar for claims (loss costs).[28] Allstate's *loss ratio*, the calculation of incurred losses divided by premiums collected, was well in line with tradition and industry averages. In 1987, Allstate paid about 71¢ out of every premium dollar for claims. By 1996, Allstate fully implemented CCPR.

By 2006, Allstate was paying only 47.6¢ per premium dollar for claims.[29] That means in 2006, Allstate was paying 23¢ less for claims than it was in 1987. That's 30% less than the 70¢ per premium dollar Allstate charges its policyholders. That's what I mean when I say Allstate is under-filling every can of insurance by 30%. It's like charging for ten ounces of protection while only providing seven ounces of coverage.

J. Robert Hunter said in a report for the Consumer Federation of America:

> The key test determining the value of insurance coverage is the benefit-to-cost ratio; incurred losses divided by premiums earned, also known in the insurance industry as the 'loss ratio.'[30]

Net pre-tax operating income figures also tell us how much of each premium dollar collected the insurer is paying out for claims. It shows how much value its policyholders are getting in return for their premium dollars. Investment analysts also look at operating income to measure an insurance company's core performance, because they can exclude investment income.[31]

Substantially increasing net operating income from premiums alone is hard for a casualty insurer to do—if it's operating the way it should. Operating the way it should means the insurer is following the traditional rules. It is charging fairly for loss costs and also paying fairly for the benefits it owes under its premiums.

Here's the story of Allstate's net pre-tax operating income between 1987 and 2006. This is not speculation. It's based on publicly reported industry financial statistics and Allstate's own stockholder reports. Between 1986 and 1995, Allstate's *total* pre-tax operating income was $820 million.[32] That's a ten-year average of $82 million a year in pre-tax operating income.

After Allstate fully implemented CCPR in 1996, that picture changed dramatically. Between 1996 and 2006, Allstate's *total* pre-tax operating income jumped to an astounding $27.4 billion.[33] That's an 11 year average of almost $2.5 *billion* a year in pre-tax operating income. That's also an incredible 3,335% increase in Allstate's average annual pre-tax operating income over the previous ten years.

What this means is that since Allstate implemented CCPR, Allstate has increased its annual average operating income by *more than 33 times*. Based on published insurance industry statistics, Allstate is the *only* insurance company that has ever managed to accomplish such an incredible increase in net operating profits. How did Allstate do it? Where did all that money come from?

Allstate's Explanation for its Earnings

News anchor Dennis Waltering, of WWL-TV in New Orleans, asked Allstate Director Rich Halberg that exact question—where did the money come from—as part of a two-part investigative report. This report aired on WWL-TV on November 6 and November 7, 2007.[34] Mr. Halberg claimed during his interview that Allstate was able to increase its operating profits by an astounding 3,335% between 1986 and 2006 by "adding millions of new customers."

This statement is technically correct, like many things Allstate tells the public. However, it's actually misleading and it doesn't answer the question. First, Allstate only provided WWL-TV with policy statistics for the years 1996 through 2006.[35] It provided no policy statistics for the years 1986 through 1995. Second, Allstate's own statistics show that between 1996 and 2006 it only increased its total number of car and homeowner policies by about 20%.[36]

According to Allstate's Proxy Statements and Annual Reports filed between 1993 and 2005, and the *Best's Review*, Allstate's car policies increased by 16%, and its homeowner policies increased by 20%.[37] These are relatively modest increases in Allstate's overall policy counts. They are just not enough to account for an increase of 3,335% in Allstate's average net operating profits. Compare its 1986 to 1995 average net income of just $82 million a year, to its average net operating profits from 1996 to 2006 of $2.5 billion per year, for an idea of the difference.

Presented graphically, the increases in the number of policies and in the net operating profits look like the following.

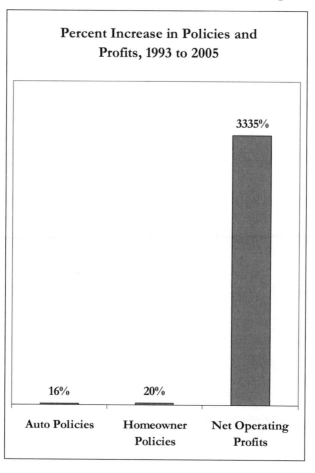

An Alternate Explanation for Allstate's Earnings

J. Robert Hunter, the Director of Insurance for the Consumer Federation of America, provides another answer to where this money came from and how Allstate managed this miraculous increase in profits over the past ten years.

> **Excessive rates and profits,** compared to the low level of claims that Allstate has paid out to consumers. *From 1987 to 1996, property-casualty insurers overall paid out 70 percent of premiums as benefits.* From 1997 to 2006, the payout was only 65%, a decline of 7.1% in value to consumers for the typical insurance product. In the late 1980s and early 1990s, Allstate's insurance products were of slightly greater value per premium dollar to consumers than those of other insurers. However, the company's property-casualty products have become less valuable than the industry average in recent years. Allstate paid out 73% of premium in benefits from 1987 to 1996 *and a startlingly low 59% from 1997 to 2006, a decline of 19.2% in the value of Allstate's product to consumers.*

> **Questionable claims settlement practices,** resulting in *unjustifiably low claims payments.* Allstate was one of the first major insurers to adopt claims payment techniques designed to systematically reduce payments to policyholders without adequately examining the validity of each individual claim, such as an automated payment system called Colossus. It adopted these techniques after being told by a consultant that these systems would put them in a "zero-sum game" with claimants, including their policyholders who filed claims, in which Allstate shareholders would benefit financially at the expense of policyholders.[38]

Unlike Allstate, the statistics Mr. Hunter cites support his answer. Mr. Hunter's answer is far more believable given the realities of today's casualty insurance industry. Allstate managed this unprecedented feat by charging excessive premiums while at the same time substantially underpaying legitimate claims. This is just what Allstate designed its CCPR system to do. The money came from the only place it *could* come from—the pockets of Allstate policyholders and claimants.

According to Allstate's publicists and lawyers, Allstate designed CCPR to stop "an historic overpayment of claims" and to curb insurance fraud. However, as the Consumer Federation of America's July 2007 report shows, *before* CCPR Allstate paid an average of 73¢ per premium dollar for claims when the overall industry average was 70¢ per premium dollar.[39] Yet, during this same period, Allstate's net profits were at least as good as, if not better than, the industry average.[40]

How do these statistics prove that Allstate or the industry *ever* had any overpayment of claims? How do they prove there was any significant insurance fraud? How could there have been an historic overpayment of claims when the rest of the industry was paying out *exactly* what it should have been charging to pay claims—70¢ per premium dollar?

In 2006, Allstate posted a $5 billion post-tax operating and investment profit.[41] That was a record for Allstate. It was also partly because Allstate's insurance companies paid out a record-low 47.6¢ per premium dollar for claims during 2006.[42] These record-breaking profits and record-low claim payments occurred despite catastrophic losses in California, Florida, and the Gulf region. In fact, ever since Allstate implemented CCPR in 1996, Allstate has bragged *every* year to the financial community about how much less it's paying for claims as compared to the industry average.[43]

Under the traditional rules we've discussed, by now we should have seen a substantial *reduction* in Allstate's premiums. Yet, just the opposite is happening. Allstate's CFO Dan Hale told investors at the USB Global Financial Services Conference on May 16, 2007, that Allstate received over 350 price increases during 2006 and planned another 300 during 2007. That makes no sense when, under what Allstate calls its "tiered" pricing structure, Allstate's premiums are already among the highest in the industry.[44]

Allstate's Story for the Public

However, that's not the story Allstate is telling the public. In 2006, at the same time it was paying out a record low 47.6¢ per premium dollar for claims, and its premiums were among the highest in the industry, Allstate ran full-page ads in national publications like *BusinessWeek* and the *New York Times.* These ads were titled "'Up in Smoke,' 'Down a Rat Hole,' and Other Misconceptions about Where Insurance Premiums Go."

At the bottom of the ad is a drawing of a man looking sorrowfully down at an open toilet bowl. The message is obvious. The text above that drawing says:

> You've been paying car insurance premiums for years. It's only natural to want to know where that money goes. We'd like to take this opportunity to tell you.
>
> **You'll be surprised to learn that most of the money insurers take in goes right back to policyholders like you.** On average, over the last five years, auto insurance companies paid out almost 75¢ in claims and related expenses for every premium dollar they took in.
>
> Obviously, after your claims are settled, there are company operations, miscellaneous expenses, and taxes. They add up to almost 24¢. **If you do the math, that means that an average of 99¢ get paid out of every dollar collected.**

So the next time you write your auto premium check, know that most of the money will go right back to consumers. **It might even go to you. That's how insurance works.**

You deserve to know where your money goes. THAT'S ALL-STATE'S STAND.[45]

While this information is true as an industry *average*, from the figures we've seen it's definitely *not* true in Allstate's case. Allstate knew that when it published the ads. However, the way Allstate worded this ad leaves the public with the false impression that Allstate was also paying out 75¢ per premium dollar for claims when it was really paying out only 47.6¢ at the time. That's "Allstate's stand" when it's talking to the public.

Allstate's Story for the Financial Community

When Allstate is talking to its investors and the financial community, however, it has quite a different story to tell. On June 1, 2006, Allstate CEO Ed Liddy made a presentation at the Sanford Bernstein & Company Strategic Decisions Conference. Liddy's presentation included a graph titled "Building a Competitive Advantage Through Claims." This graph compares Allstate's actual claim and expense payouts against the industry average since 1995 for the four separate casualty coverages it sells: Bodily Injury, Property Damage, Collision, and Homeowners.

In each type of coverage, especially the car coverages, the graphs show that Allstate's average claim payments have remained substantially lower than the industry's average every year since Allstate implemented CCPR. A display taken directly from Allstate's web site shows what Liddy used to extol his strategic decisions to his fellow CEOs.[46]

The slide on Allstate's site showed the following four graphs combined into one slide.

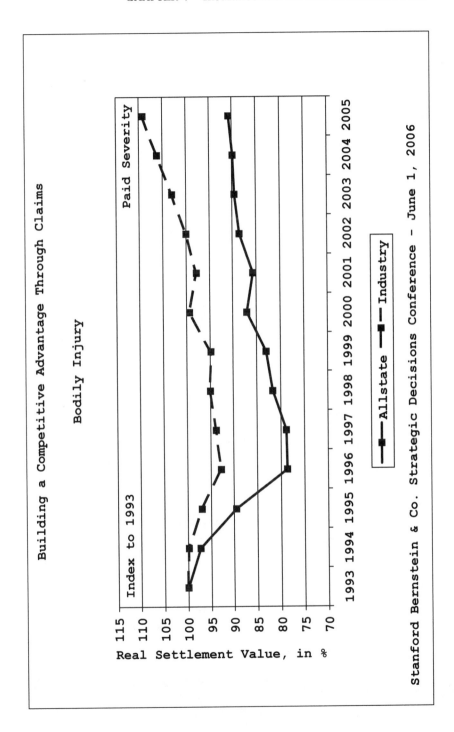

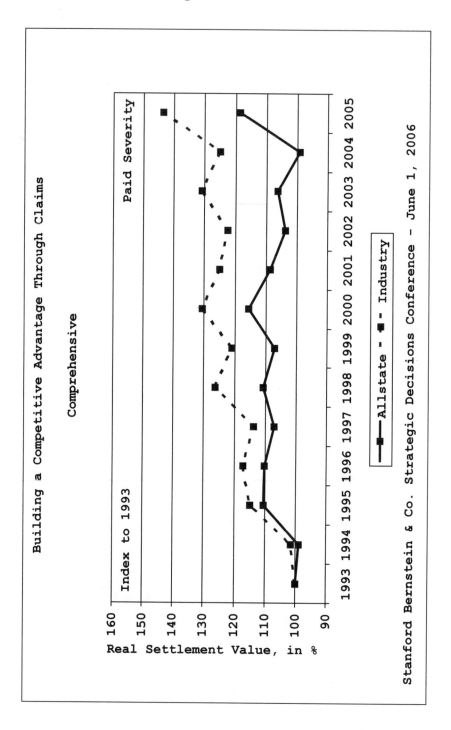

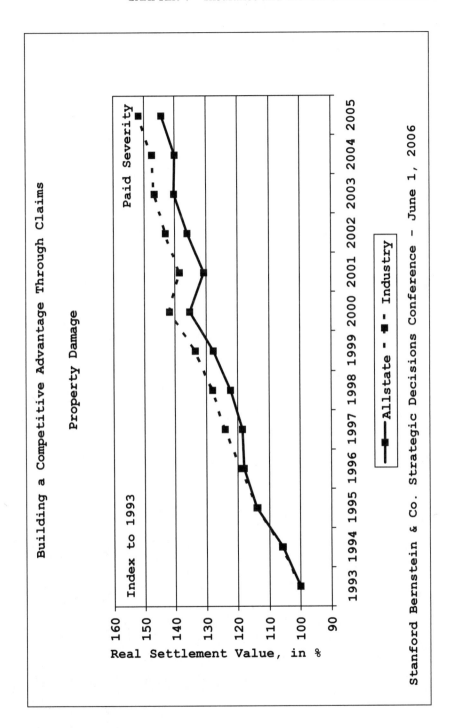

Building a Competitive Advantage Through Claims

Property Damage

Paid Severity

Stanford Bernstein & Co. Strategic Decisions Conference – June 1, 2006

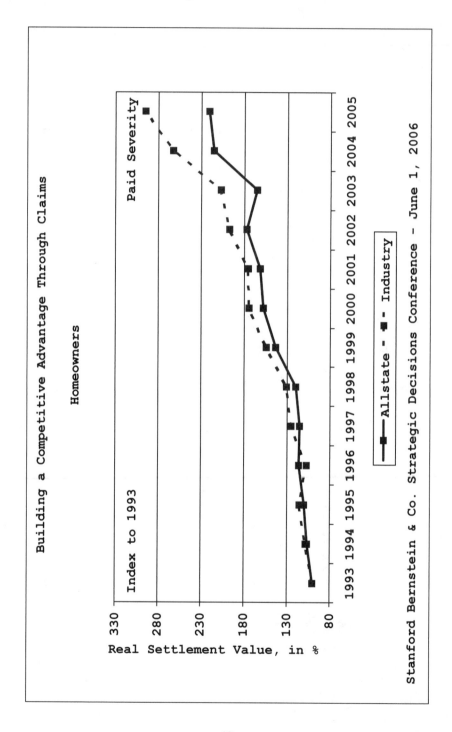

As these graphs show, at the same time Allstate was implying to the public it was paying 75¢ per premium dollar for auto claims, Mr. Liddy was bragging to the investment community that Allstate was really paying out less than 50¢—about 30% less than the average for the rest of the industry. These are typical examples of how Allstate deals with the public in the post-McKinsey era.

If Allstate were selling peas, you'd call it fraud to charge customers for ten ounces after deliberately setting the machinery at their factory to under-fill every can by three ounces. However, that's not how Allstate's executive officers describe what it's doing in presentations to its shareholders. Allstate's executives tell their shareholders that Allstate is "Building a Competitive Advantage Through Claims."[47] The only problem with this statement is that it is directly contrary to what we've seen are the rules of insurer conduct.

We can also prove Allstate's consistent underpayment of claims by looking at what McKinsey's business model has done for Allstate's surplus since 1996. As I've explained earlier, surplus means an insurer's net worth in ordinary accounting terms. Insurance executives consider growing surplus to be the most important part of an insurance enterprise.

What happened to Allstate's surplus after it adopted McKinsey's business model? It skyrocketed from $6.5 billion in 1994 to $21.8 billion in 2006.[48] That's a total increase of $15.3 billion in just 12 years. That means Allstate increased its surplus by an average of $1.2 billion per year. In comparison, between 1986 and 1994 (the nine years immediately before CCPR), Allstate's surplus increased by a total of just $2.5 billion. That's an average yearly increase of only $277 million.[49]

The graph on the next pages shows Allstate's surplus between 1986 and 2005.[50] It hovers around $4 billion from 1986 to 1993, and then in 1995 after Allstate implemented CCPR, it begins to climb.

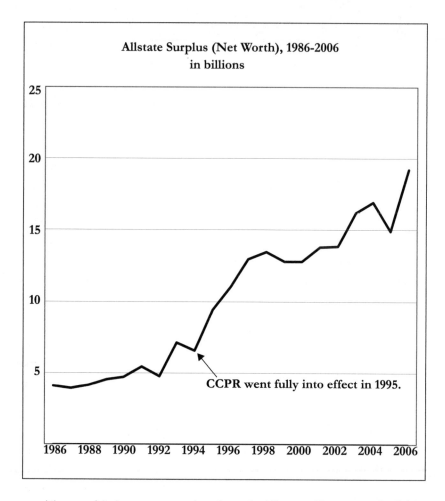

Allstate Surplus (Net Worth), 1986-2006
in billions

CCPR went fully into effect in 1995.

To put this into perspective, it took Allstate 63 years to build its 1994 surplus to $6.5 billion.[51] Yet, after adopting McKinsey's business model, Allstate more than tripled its surplus in only 12 years. That's even more remarkable because Allstate is telling the financial community that since 1996 it has paid out 74% of its net income to shareholders.[52]

Surplus grows when an insurer transfers net income into its surplus. That means Allstate has been able to increase its surplus by an average of $1.2 billion a year since 1996 using only 26% of its annual net income. It also means that since 1996 Allstate has probably paid approximately $25 billion to its shareholders. Again, unlike what Allstate told the public in its 2006 ad about car insurance premiums, a large part of the premium money Allstate pays out seems to be going to its shareholders, not its policyholders.

Allstate's explanations for why it implemented CCPR and how it managed its phenomenal financial success raise lots of questions. What's Allstate's explanation for reducing its claim payments again in 2006, *after* Hurricane Katrina (August 2005), to a shocking 47.6¢ per premium dollar?[53] What's Allstate's explanation for paying an *average* of only 59¢ per premium dollar for claims between 1996 to 2006 while still charging its policyholders about 70¢ per premium dollar for loss costs?[54] Why has Allstate requested over 650 price increases during the past two years while "most insurers are lowering prices" and while Allstate already charges some of the highest premiums in the industry?[55]

Why has Allstate cancelled or refused to renew homeowner policies for millions of families in Connecticut, California, Delaware, Florida, Maryland, New York, Texas, Virginia, and Washington State?[56] Finally, in light of its low-risk business model, record high profits, and record low claim payments, why is Allstate now slashing its coverages to eliminate coverage for many of the important losses its policyholders have come to expect coverage for?[57]

Did Allstate design CCPR to address "a historic overpayment of claims"? Or did they design CCPR, as Allstate's phenomenal profits over the past ten years suggest, to produce stupendous wealth for its shareholders and executives?

5

McKinsey and the "Greed is Good" Model

T O UNDERSTAND the McKinsey slides, it's also helpful to know something about McKinsey, its personnel, and its methodology. McKinsey has a long history as an advisor to the world's top corporations.[58] Secretive and seemingly all powerful, some call McKinsey the Jesuits of the business world—an elite order of business disciples steeped in a powerful corporate culture of mystery, rigorous training, and absolute allegiance to a monolithic code of business principles.[59]

Much of the McKinsey mystique arises from its fabled and mostly secret formulas for solving the problems of the world's wealthiest corporations.[60] A lot of McKinsey's success happens for reasons that are more mundane. It comes from an intense focus on the bottom line—how to devise outcomes that make an immediate impact on profits.

McKinsey recruits from the elite of the elite, the top graduates of the best business and law schools in the world.[61] Many top business school graduates actively seek McKinsey employment. They know from history that a stint at McKinsey can open many corporate doors—including the one to the CEO's suite.[62] Many notable McKinsey alumni have achieved the highest international success and acclaim in their professional endeavors after leaving the company.[63]

One McKinsey alumnus achieved international notoriety of a different sort. He is Jeffrey Skilling, an MBA graduate of the Harvard Business School and former "superstar" McKinsey partner who became the CEO of Enron in 1996.[64] At Enron, McKinsey's "greed is good" credo was never more devoutly embraced. This is not surprising given the influence of both McKinsey and Skilling at Enron.

McKinsey and Enron

Enron imported Jeff Skilling from McKinsey to shape Enron's corporate strategies and guide the company to a bigger and brighter future. Unfortunately, Skilling's aggressive business initiatives backfired for both Enron and thousands of its employees and stockholders.

Described by colleagues in a February 2002 *BusinessWeek* article as a "brilliant strategist," Skilling "embodied the in-your-face Enron culture, where risk taking, deal making, and 'thinking outside the box' were richly rewarded, while controls appeared loose at best."[65]

This same *BusinessWeek* article reported that a number of ex-employees said Skilling was turning Enron into a "rogue company" that was "determined to pump its stock and make earnings [net profits] at any price." Skilling's philosophy of thinking outside the box to devise strategic initiatives that increase net earnings and shareholder value seems to be a defining element of McKinsey's approach to business.

On August 18, 2001, Mr. Skilling stepped down as Chairman and CEO of Enron amid mounting public questions about Enron's financial statements. On September 17, 2001, Mr. Skilling sold over

$60 million in personal Enron stock. He claimed he did so because he feared a stock crash after the September 11 terrorist attacks—not because he knew Enron was about to collapse.

After a 16-week trial and 56 days of testimony, Mr. Skilling was convicted on May 26, 2006, of nineteen counts of conspiracy, fraud, false statements, and insider trading.[66] Jurors didn't seem to respond well to his defense that he did nothing wrong because he always acted to benefit Enron's shareholders. The McKinsey slides echo the theme of Mr. Skilling's business philosophy—and his criminal defense.

McKinsey's Methods

Part of McKinsey's methodology drilled into every consultant is to always question *why* the client does a certain business procedure they way they do, and to try new, innovative, and perhaps even radical alternatives to that methodology. To "think outside the box."[67]

McKinsey also puts great emphasis during its engagements on exhorting its clients' senior executives to fully embrace its "do whatever it takes" ethic. Using this ethic, McKinsey's clients can reengineer their business processes to quickly increase net profits and shareholder values. "Do whatever it takes" is just another way of saying "greed is good"—the Enron business model.

At Enron, the executives working under Skilling enthusiastically embraced the "greed is good" ethic. Under Skilling's leadership, Enron matured into an acclaimed role-model for a McKinsey-inspired corporate culture that swept through the highest circles of America's senior corporate management. Some commentators in the post-Enron era have labeled it "the culture of greed." Despite the huge amount of discredit heaped on this business model, the evidence shows it's still alive and well at Allstate.

One of the principal tools McKinsey installed at both Enron and Allstate was executive performance incentives. Under McKinsey's model for success, both companies rewarded senior executives who embraced the approach with incentives that could easily reach $10 million per year.

McKinsey's connection to Enron and its culture goes much deeper than former partner Jeffrey Skilling. As a corporate advisor to Enron for nearly eighteen years, "McKinsey was the key architect of strategic thinking" at Enron. At times, McKinsey's consultants even sat in on Enron's board of directors meetings.[68]

In fact, McKinsey was not only the creator of the Enron business model and its "greed is good" credo, but also an ardent and influential advocate for it. Throughout the 1990's, especially during the time McKinsey was engaged in redesigning Allstate's practices, McKinsey also enthusiastically marketed its business model to the corporate world.

McKinsey's top partners "eagerly promoted" the "underlying principles of Enron's transformation" and "regularly stamped their imprimatur on many of Enron's strategies and practices" in books, articles and essays. Before its collapse, McKinsey's high profile partners routinely held up Enron to its clients as "a corporate innovator worthy of emulation" and a business model for how to generate phenomenal jumps in profits quickly.[69]

The McKinsey slides show McKinsey advising and encouraging Allstate's top executives to adopt its widely praised business model. Motivated by McKinsey's promises of record profits in record time and large executive bonuses, Allstate's executives turned their backs on the traditional insurance rules. They eagerly embraced McKinsey's template for redesigning the company's practices.

As we've seen, McKinsey's model more than performed as promised at Allstate. It surpassed anything Allstate's executives might have dared to hope for. McKinsey created stupendous results for themselves and Allstate's shareholders—and equally disastrous results for Allstate's policyholders.[70]

Another defining characteristic of McKinsey's problem-solving methodology has been its ability to develop a relatively small number of robust formulas or tools. McKinsey's consultants then rapidly adapt these formulas to a large number of seemingly unrelated businesses.[71] This has led some to criticism McKinsey for basing its business solutions on "pre-canned" or "cookie cutter" formulas.[72]

Whether or not this criticism is valid, it is true that in late 1990 McKinsey was completing development of a new problem-solving tool called Business Process Redesign (BPR).[73] By 1992, McKinsey adapted its BPR formula into a new tool called Core Process Redesign, or CPR.

The CPR Formula

Two Harvard Business School professors appear to have inspired the theories McKinsey used in its CPR formula, in their 1990 *Harvard Business Review* article, "Core Competence of the Corporation."[74] Given its name and use during the Allstate project, it looks like McKinsey designed CPR to give its teams a formula to pick out a client's core skills and chief strategic market intent. The McKinsey team would then redesign a unique set of business processes that would "dramatically and rapidly increase shareholder value, as measured by improved cash flow and share price."

McKinsey's presentations during the CCPR design project urged Allstate's executives to embrace the idea that management's top priority should be producing rapid and dramatic increases in profits. To do this, Allstate's management also needed to make this the top priority of *every* new business practice at Allstate. This meant CCPR would have to build entirely on those practices which produced the largest increase in profits in the shortest time.

In the 1980s and 1990s, McKinsey worked on a number of projects for major insurance companies seeking to increase their profits. These included State Farm, United Services Automobile Association (USAA), Liberty Mutual, and apparently Hartford and

Nationwide as well.[75] During the mid-1980s, USAA invited interested insurance companies and their claim executives to its home office in San Antonio for open discussions about how McKinsey redesigned its claim system. USAA credited McKinsey with saving the company. It openly shared information about McKinsey's redesign with its competitors.[76]

McKinsey apparently chooses special names for its engagements based on the formula it uses as its model for the project. For example, McKinsey named its USAA project PACE, Professionalism and Claims Excellence. McKinsey named its State Farm redesign project ACE, Advancing Claims Excellence.[77]

Nationwide also has ACE, but it is rumored to mean Accelerating Claims Excellence. Farmers, which McKinsey redesigned with ideas that migrated to Accenture, called its program ACME, Advancing Claims Management Expertise. This similarity in names suggests McKinsey's use of a similar problem-solving formula during each of these engagements.

McKinsey's name for the Allstate project, Claim Core Process Redesign, was a clear departure from the names given to its prior insurance projects. This new name implies not just a new approach, but also the use of a new tool in its intellectual toolbox—its Core Process Redesign tool—as its problem-solving formula for Allstate. At the beginning of the Allstate engagement in 1992 and 1993, McKinsey repeatedly referred to the project as CPR or Core Process Redesign. By 1994 and 1995, the project name had changed to CCPR, or Claim Core Process Redesign.

The McKinsey slides show disturbing similarities between their new approach to both Allstate and Enron, and some equally disturbing differences. At Enron, "greed is good" produced a colossal collapse for Enron's shareholders, and criminal convictions for Enron's executives. McKinsey's approach at Enron cost that company's shareholders about $68 billion—against a backdrop of a national media frenzy, books, and documentary movies.[78]

The CPR Formula at Allstate

At Allstate, "greed is good" produced colossal riches for Allstate's shareholders and executives. Yet Allstate's approach poses risks of greater losses for most Americans who depend on the insurance system for their financial security. Why the difference?

Until recently, there has been near total apathy about insurance on the part of the national media, regulators, and the courts. With no corporate transparency, and no perceived need to get permission from regulators or the courts, Allstate and McKinsey have slid their programs in under everyone's radar—until now. The aftermath of Katrina may be a major wake-up call.

What kind of market are we talking about? In 2004 alone, the net earned premiums taken in by the casualty insurance industry grew to $412.6 billion. The industry's total assets reached a staggering $1.183 trillion. To put that in perspective, that's over a third of President Bush's proposed $2.77 trillion federal budget for 2007.[79]

Claim payments are supposed to represent around 70% of those 2004 net premiums. That means for 2004 the casualty insurance industry should be holding about $300 billion in the premium-paying public's joint claims account. That's supposed to be a trust fund earmarked for the full payment of claims. In addition, this fund isn't dead money—it's increasing every year by an average of about $23 billion.[80]

Suppose the McKinsey slides reflect a future where, in order to remain competitive, every insurer must follow Allstate's example. The premium-paying public could end up spending as much as $100 billion every year for casualty coverage that insurers have no intention of paying. In just ten years, the cost to the public for this illusory insurance could top $1 trillion—a number that would make the $68 billion Enron collapse look insignificant by comparison.

Since Enron's collapse, questions have arisen about McKinsey's accountability for the strategic thinking that turned Enron's senior executives from Wall Street darlings to convicted criminals.[81] Public revelation of McKinsey's role in Allstate's CCPR should lead to similar questions, not only about McKinsey's role at Allstate, but also about the damage CCPR is spreading through the American insurance system. We enable these corporations to serve us in a vital role, but they don't do that very well. Should we allow them to continue?

In the end, the story of CCPR and its radical departure from the traditional rules of insurance isn't just about Allstate. It's also about McKinsey. It's a story about the power and influence of an invisible hand guiding insurance ethics that now threaten the financial safety net for the American public.

This story should raise hard questions about the practices of the world's preeminent business consultant. Was it ethical for McKinsey to secretly introduce its "greed is good" culture into the insurance industry? McKinsey knew this industry was built on rules that expressly forbid insurers from placing their interest in profits above the interests of policyholders. Was it ethical for Allstate to go along with what McKinsey suggested, knowing they violate traditional insurance laws? How can profits be more important than providing the vital public service the insurance industry was created to deliver?

6

From Sears to CCPR

A Golden Opportunity for Executive Wealth

A LLSTATE AND its original parent, Sears, Roebuck & Company, have long relationships with America. Sears built its business on two revolutionary retail innovations of the early 1900s: mass mail-order marketing through catalogs, and Sears's famous "satisfaction guaranteed—money-back" promise.

These innovations helped build an enormous financial empire fueled by the previously untapped buying power of mostly rural Americans. This success in turn propelled Sears into urban markets using traditional stores.

Allstate at the World's Fair: 1933

Sears founded Allstate in 1931 as its mail-order insurance division. During the 1933 Chicago World's Fair, Sears put an Allstate agent at a card table in a corner of its exhibit. Drawn by their trust in Sears's "satisfaction guaranteed" reputation, customers mobbed the agent. Allstate was the hit of the Fair.

The overwhelming response at the World's Fair convinced Sears to put Allstate agents in booths in its stores—usually under the escalator, long considered the least valuable space on the sales floor. Allstate built its customer base on the strong relationship—and trust—developed over the years between Sears and its customers. Sears created Allstate's motto, "You're In Good Hands," to convey the same idea that built Sears into an American retailing icon: "satisfaction guaranteed." Allstate built its business on that motto, and that was how Allstate operated, until it hired McKinsey.

Allstate Hires McKinsey: 1992

One thing the McKinsey slides don't tell us is exactly what prompted Allstate's executive managers to turn to McKinsey for its legendary problem-solving assistance in 1992. They also don't tell us who among Allstate's top executives came up with the idea to call on McKinsey.[82]

We know Allstate contacted McKinsey in 1992, and not the other way around. McKinsey doesn't approach clients about doing engagements for them. Clients who want its service must come to McKinsey first. So, why did Allstate call McKinsey at that particular time? That could answer many questions: why Allstate agreed to adopt McKinsey's business model, and what the motives of its top executives were at the time.

We know approximately when Allstate contacted McKinsey. One McKinsey slide refers to a September 3, 1992 planning session between the McKinsey team and Allstate's finance department. However, the slide doesn't tell us the purpose of this meeting. McKinsey's initial presentation slides bear a document identification code "00324091092." This suggests McKinsey started creating the slides for its initial presentation on September 10, 1992 (091092). From the dates on the final version, it appears McKinsey made its initial presentation to Allstate's senior executives on September 28, 1992.

Before the McKinsey consulting team could meet with Allstate's finance department or create slides for its initial presentation, many other things had to happen. First, Allstate would have to contact McKinsey. Then there would be preliminary discussions about what Allstate wanted from McKinsey. The scope and scale of Allstate's goals would be essential to McKinsey's development of its proposals for the project. Then, of course, both McKinsey and Allstate's senior management would have to agree on the financial arrangements for the engagement.

Next, McKinsey would have to designate a team leader and assemble the right available consultants. The team and its leader would in turn have to meet for preliminary discussions to formulate their "initial hypothesis." An initial hypothesis is McKinsey's definition of Allstate's problem and McKinsey's proposed solutions. This would involve research, such as a review of other insurance projects from McKinsey's vast library about the businesses and industries of its clients. This would all take time; perhaps weeks, maybe months.

Only then would the McKinsey team be able to start crafting the all-important initial presentation to Allstate's key senior executives. If McKinsey's engagement team didn't start preparing its initial presentation until September 10, 1992, this would suggest Allstate's initial contact with McKinsey must have been in July or August 1992, perhaps earlier.

The financial literature from that time reveals the purpose of McKinsey's CPR (Core Process Redesign) formula was to redesign core business processes to rapidly increase profits and shareholder value. Businesses who wanted this kind of help were usually in a financial crisis, even if the crisis was not in the immediate future.

Was Allstate facing an immediate financial crisis in the summer of 1992? The answer is clearly, "no." Allstate would post a loss for the year of $825 million, no small amount by any measure, but $300 million of that loss seems to have been a "paper loss" caused by an accounting adjustment from prior accounting periods.[83]

Another unique reason for Allstate's negative income for 1992 was Hurricane Andrew, the Category 5 hurricane that hit south Florida on August 24, 1992. At the time, Andrew was the most destructive catastrophe in history to hit the continental United States. It damaged or destroyed 85,000 houses, 38,000 apartments, and almost 11,000 mobile homes, causing $16 billion in covered insurance losses.[84] No one would know the full extent of that damage for many months—and certainly not in July or August of 1992.

Still, Allstate's surplus at the end 1992 was a solid $5.3 billion.[85] In 1993, Allstate posted a net profit of $1.3 billion using its old systems. A severe financial crisis doesn't seem to be the reason for senior management's sudden desire to commission the most expensive corporate consultant in the world to completely redesign their business.

We also know that Allstate had just invested substantial time and money, both at the home office and in the field, to design and implement its own significant overhaul of its claim processes. This new claim system, implemented on July 1, 1992, involved a new bodily injury reporting system called the *C1097 Injury Evaluation Form*.[86] By mid-September 1992, there would hardly have been time to fully implement this new claim process, let alone determine its success.

Why then would Allstate's senior executives feel the need to go further into redesigning its claim-handling system again, and so soon? They would have known that calling in McKinsey usually means a full-blown redesign of all the company's business processes starting from scratch. This would be an enormously difficult and expensive undertaking for a large organization.[87]

It would not be something Allstate's executives would undertake lightly. Something big must have been happening at Allstate in the first half of 1992—and it wasn't Hurricane Andrew. Would any other business events involving Allstate explain its sudden call to McKinsey?

Allstate's Split from Sears: 1994

The answer probably has to do with what was happening at Sears. In the early 1990s, Sears was the sole shareholder in four major business entities: Sears Merchandise Group, Allstate Insurance Group, Dean Witter-Discover Financial Services Group, and Coldwell Banker Real Estate Group. Under financial pressure to prop up the flagging performance of Sears Merchandise Group, Sears apparently decided sometime during 1992 on a major restructuring of its business operations, set to occur in 1994 or 1995.[88]

Sears wanted to return to its retailing roots, and planned to raise capital by selling off its three wholly-owned subsidiaries: Allstate, Coldwell Banker, and Dean Witter-Discover. The spin-off would be the two largest initial public offerings (IPOs) up to that point in Wall Street history. In early 1993, Sears completed the IPO of 20% of its Dean Witter-Discover stock. In the second-largest stock dividend distribution in Wall Street history, Sears then spun off its remaining shares of Dean Witter-Discover to Sears's shareholders.[89]

In 1994, Sears set another financial milestone with the IPO of 20% of its Allstate stock—then the largest insurance company IPO in Wall Street history. Sears distributed the remaining Allstate stock to Sears's shareholders on June 3, 1995. Sears had created three separate, publicly-owned, and non-affiliated companies: Allstate, Dean Witter-Discover, and Coldwell Banker.[90]

Sears didn't make the official announcement of its restructuring plan until January 1993. However, word of the Sears plan may well have reached the senior executives at Allstate by the summer of 1992. There is no way of knowing today who tipped off Allstate's executives to Sears's then-secret restructuring plan.

In the summer of 1992, Sears's Chief Financial Officer (CFO) was Edward Liddy. Two years after Sears' official announcement in January 1993, Liddy left his position as Senior Vice President and CFO of Sears to become President and CEO of Allstate Corporation, the holding company of all the Allstate brand insurance companies.[91] This made him second in command to Allstate's Chairman of the Board Jerry Choate.[92] Liddy replaced Choate as Chairman in 1999 when Choate retired.

The financial opportunity for executive wealth building which Sears's anticipated business plans represented could hardly have been lost on Allstate's senior executives in the summer of 1992— or on Liddy. The compensation plan for Allstate's executives had long included Sears stock and options.[93] However, the value of their Sears stock depended on the overall financial performance of all four separate businesses, three of which they had no control over. That included the worst performer in the group, Sears itself.

Sears's decision meant this was all about to change. Allstate would become the nation's largest publicly-traded personal lines insurance company.[94] Independence from Sears would mean the value of Allstate's stock—and the stock options of its executive officers—would depend solely on Allstate's ability to increase net profits and build value of Allstate stock.

Executive Wealth and the Allstate IPO

The Allstate IPO would have provided any astute Allstate executive an ideal opportunity, and strong incentives, to adopt McKinsey's business model. This was precisely the time when McKinsey's model could give a top Allstate executive one of the greatest opportunities for personal wealth-building in the company's history.

McKinsey's CPR formula for rapidly increasing corporate profits relied heavily on financial rewards for employees. These rewards encouraged acceptance of the major changes in business operations this formula always produced.

The CPR formula also relied on large stock bonuses and options for the company's top executives as incentives for attaining goals and boosting stock performance. One of the principal tools

McKinsey used at both Enron and Allstate to drive obsessive pursuit of increased profits, regardless of consequences to the customer, was executive performance incentives.

McKinsey's extensive use of financial incentives for employees and options for executives guarantees that the interests of employees and management are aligned with those of shareholders. McKinsey designed this business model to make Allstate's shareholders and its top executives the primary beneficiaries of the CCPR system it would install at Allstate.

Proof of McKinsey's plan to put the shareholders ahead of Allstate's policyholders isn't hard to find. Allstate's 2005 Proxy Statement clearly spells out this plan.[95]

> Because *we believe strongly in linking the interests of management with those of our shareholders,* we first instituted stock ownership goals in 1996 for executives at the vice president level and above. These goals were revised in 2004 to require these executives to own, within five years of the date the executive position is assumed, common stock worth a multiple of base salary:
>
> | | |
> |---|---|
> | Chief Executive Officer | *7 times salary* |
> | Senior Management Executives | *4 times salary* |
> | Other Executives | *2 times salary* |

According to Allstate's 2007 proxy statement, Allstate's current CEO Thomas Wilson received total compensation of $7,831,055 for 2006. Seven times that amount would be over $50 million, meaning Wilson could be required to own over $50 million in Allstate stock within five years of January 1, 2007 in order to keep his job.

If you had a $50 million investment in Allstate stock, whose interests would you be more interested in protecting: shareholders or policyholders? Whose interests do you think Mr. Wilson and the other senior Allstate executives subject to such a stock ownership plan are more likely to be interested in protecting? As one McKinsey slide states, "[Our] Customers [are our] Shareholders."

The McKinsey slides show Allstate drove its CCPR project from the top down. In 1992, one senior Allstate executive who might have appreciated the opportunity for personal financial gain was Jerry Choate, Senior Executive Vice President of Claims.

At that time, Choate was president of Allstate's all-important business division, Personal Property & Casualty (PP&C),[96] and the heir apparent to become Allstate's new President and CEO after the Sears IPO. In August 1994, Choate finally did become Allstate's new President and CEO.[97]

The McKinsey slides don't say directly who was behind All-state's decision to hire McKinsey in the summer of 1992. However, we know Choate was the President of the PP&C executive management team for claims to whom McKinsey made its initial presentation on September 28, 1992. That strongly suggests Choate also played a major role in hiring McKinsey. Other information in the McKinsey slides also suggests Choate was a driving force behind bringing McKinsey to Allstate for the CCPR project.

Choate was a top name on the list of members for two of McKinsey's Performance Initiative Subteams, which started the CCPR project. The slides also contain a "CCPR Family Tree," with Choate's name at the top and all teams and projects operating under him. The slides state that Choate personally approved many CCPR initiatives and the outlines of many McKinsey presentations.

The McKinsey slides also suggest a direct link between the creation of CCPR and the Sears IPO, at least in the mind of one unnamed senior executive at Allstate. In a memo dated November 17, 1993 and entitled "Incentive Compensation 1994—Claim Core Process Redesign—IPO," the unidentified author outlines the following.

INCENTIVE COMPENSATION 1994
Claim Core Process Redesign—IPO

Auto Homeowner Outcomes:

Completion of all data collection
Hypothesis defined
Process maps for proposed organization
    developed

Threshold   Target   Maximum
80% Completion   90% Completion   100% Completion

In addition to the bonus level members receiving the 10% IPO, I would like to give the non-
bonus level members an opportunity to earn a
performance bonus on the same objectives. The
potential non-bonus level awards would be as
follows:

Threshold   Target   Maximum
1,000   2,000   3,000

[handwritten] 4 people: Carolyn, Ken, Pam, Paul
3000 x 4 = 12,000 max[98]

The slides don't tell us if Allstate enacted this bonus plan. We do know that Choate and Liddy immediately implemented McKinsey's recommendation to create executive compensation plans at Allstate based on a strong belief in "linking the interests of management with those of our shareholders." Together, Choate and Liddy used the Sears IPO, and their adoption of McKinsey's business plan, to create lottery-sized personal fortunes for themselves.

By December 31, 1997, Choate owned Allstate stock and options totaling over 700,000 shares and worth an estimated $63,000,000.[99] After engineering an Allstate stock split in July 1998, Choate retired from Allstate effective December 31, 1998 with a retirement package worth an additional approximately $10 million.[100]

At the time of his retirement on December 31, 2006, Liddy owned 3,823,255 shares of Allstate stock, worth approximately $250,000,000 at the market price of $65.11.[101] This is in addition to about $20 million he received for selling some of his Allstate stock between August 2004 and August 2005, and another $16 million from his sale of Allstate stock in 2006.

On top of this, Allstate's 2007 Proxy statement reports that on December 31, 2006, Liddy received approximately $50 million in "Amounts Immediately Payable Upon Effective Date of Change-in-Control."[102] Last, but hardly least, Allstate's 2007 Proxy Statement states that in four years Liddy will receive his retirement package, which looks to be worth roughly $71 million.[103]

In all, Liddy's move to Allstate in 1994 netted a personal fortune of approximately $350 million upon his retirement on December 31, 2006—much of it due directly to McKinsey's business model.

Of course, the fruits of McKinsey's labors at Allstate would not be limited to Allstate's executives and employees. Allstate's senior management adopted CCPR for the express benefit of Allstate's shareholders who have reaped billions in stock dividends in the process. As stated earlier, Allstate's shareholders have received about $19 billion since 1996, according to Allstate V.P. Robert Block's presentation on November 13, 2006 to the 2007 Argus-Vision financial conference.[104]

Lost and forgotten in McKinsey's business model (and in the rush by Allstate's senior executives to cash in on the Sears IPO) was the group of people for whose benefit Allstate was supposed to be operating—the premium-paying policyholders. For them, McKinsey's business model has meant only two things: excessive premiums combined with drastically reduced claim payments.

7

McKinsey's Initial
Presentation

T HREE SEEMS to be McKinsey's magic number.[105] McKinsey usually divides its engagements into three phases:

1. Formulating and presenting the initial hypothesis.

2. Proving and designing the initial hypothesis.

3. Testing, improving, and implementing the initial hypothesis.[106]

Every McKinsey engagement is based on problem solving.[107] McKinsey's initial hypothesis defines both the client's problem and McKinsey's solution for that problem before the engagement even begins.[108] Preparations for the initial presentation to the client center on formulating McKinsey's initial hypothesis.[109] The initial presentation essentially defines the problem for the client in McKinsey's terms and then sells McKinsey's solutions to the client.

Naturally, there are three reasons McKinsey can do this.

- McKinsey has nearly a century of experience solving the problems of the world's largest corporations. They've seen, analyzed, and solved just about every problem corporate clients usually face.

- McKinsey's most valuable asset is information. Since the 1920s, McKinsey has stockpiled the information and analyses about every imaginable type of business; information McKinsey never discards. This has allowed it to build what is likely the most diverse, highly developed, and sophisticated database of information about various types of businesses in the world.[110] McKinsey always has a head start. It relies on its extensive fund of relevant data about the workings of its clients' businesses, and the industries in which they compete, before it starts the engagement.

- As we've seen, McKinsey's years of experience have enabled it to devise a number of proven solutions that it can tailor to any client's problem.

These are the reasons McKinsey teams can supply both the problem's identity and its solution during the initial presentation. McKinsey has usually seen and successfully solved the same problem before for another client. This experience and insight form a large part of what many call the *McKinsey Mystique*.

Formulating the initial hypothesis involves a process McKinsey calls "structuring" the engagement.[111] That process sets out the objectives, targets, and milestones of the intended project within the constraints of the client's budget, and the capacity of the team that will complete the work.[112] Usually, an Engagement Director or Director of Client Services structures the engagement.[113]

The engagement leader assembles the team and holds preliminary meetings—brainstorming sessions—at which the team members come up with the initial hypothesis based on experience and research. Then, McKinsey makes its first presentation to the client.

This involves laying out the hypothesis, objectives, and methodology in order to sell the client on the engagement.[114]

No Surprises From McKinsey

McKinsey teams don't surprise their clients during the initial presentation. The team pre-wires everything with the relevant players in advance.[115] For the Allstate engagement, it's safe to assume McKinsey met with the key Allstate PP&C (Personal Property and Casualty) executives such as Jerry Choate, Robert Gary, and Bill Dixon before the initial presentation. It's safe to assume the McKinsey team obtained full agreement with their findings and recommendations from Allstate's top managers before its initial presentation.

The senior Allstate executives attending McKinsey's first presentation on September 28, 1992 had a lot at stake. The McKinsey team was selling a top-to-bottom redesign that would take six to eight years, and probably cost Allstate over a quarter of a billion dollars in McKinsey fees alone.[116]

To Allstate's PP&C management team, this was much more than a total restructuring of Allstate's business operations. The team's decision to use McKinsey's plan would determine how Allstate would operate as an independent company. This decision would also have a direct impact on matters of great personal concern to these men. These matters included the value of future executive pay plans, the value of retirement plans, and an unparalleled opportunity for personal wealth building.

The management team already knew that Allstate stock options and rewards would play a critical role in McKinsey's plan. These were high stakes—a big gamble for executives not used to taking risks. However, by this time, McKinsey had already started its ACE engagement for State Farm, the largest insurer in the country—the only insurer bigger than Allstate.

McKinsey started its initial presentation by comparing the *combined ratios* for State Farm (103.4) and Allstate (104.9) for 1992. Combined ratio is the relationship of all the expenses of an insurance company (including claim payments) compared to written premiums. If a company takes in a dollar and pays out a dollar, that's a combined ratio of 100.0. Insurers get to invest the premiums they've collected for the year and haven't paid out yet as well as what's left over. Depending on the quality of its investments, an insurer can make a return of anywhere between 5% and 10% on that money. A combined ratio goal would establish targets for measuring the Allstate's business processes. McKinsey used State Farm's performance as the target.[117] It then set a combined ratio goal of 103.9 for Allstate in 1996.

McKinsey's engagement at Allstate would be different from its prior insurance company engagements. This would be McKinsey's first use of its new CPR problem-solving tool on a complete redesign of an insurer's claim processes. At the initial presentation, McKinsey described its new CPR formula and how they would use it during the engagement to sell its new tool to Allstate's management.

The rough outline of McKinsey's plan to increase profits by redesigning Allstate's claims factory to under-fill every can of Allstate insurance is in several slides from McKinsey's initial presentation. The first slide is entitled "Issues For Claims Redesign."

Issues For Claims Redesign

Overall Objective:
    Redesign activities and core processes to
    significantly improve Allstate's competi-
    tive economics over the intermediate and
    longer time period.

Claims Objective:
    Improve execution and optimize balance of
    severities and expenses *to minimize total*

How can Allstate reduce overpayment by better
standardizing best practices in all phases of
file execution across the 10,000 claim repre-
sentatives?

Can Allstate improve its litigation management
across the many different local markets and
thousands of front-line decisions made daily
(e.g., to limit retention of attorneys/filing
of suit, build claim department litigation management skills and decision support, effectively deploy staff counsel and manage outside
counsel)?

Do claims reps possess adequate technical
expertise for effective medical management
... to ensure treatment appropriateness and
exercise medical cost containment?

What opportunities exist to reduce expenses by
automation/technology...?

Are there economically justified opportunities
for investment in expenses *to drive greater
reduction in severities*?[118]

The CPR formula was "a targeted program" designed to achieve "substantial improvement in performance" through reconfiguring business activities and information flows that are sufficiently broad to encompass one or more core processes.

The only legitimate measure of performance under McKinsey's business model is increased profits. Thus, as the slide on page 71 states, the "Overall Objective" of CPR would be to "redesign activities and core processes to significantly improve Allstate's competitive economics over the immediate and longer time period."

The CPR "Claims Objective" would be to "improve execution and optimize [the] balance of severities and expenses to minimize [the] total." Keep in mind that "severities" refers to the average claim payments. McKinsey meant to minimize them.

A secondary CPR objective would be to maximize customer satisfaction "to the extent economically feasible." Perhaps McKinsey meant that if policyholders wanted both fair *and* prompt payment, customer satisfaction would not be "economically feasible."

McKinsey's Solution to Allstate's Problem

By framing the question as "how can Allstate reduce overpayment" of claims, McKinsey defined Allstate's problem and suggested the solution would involve transferring the most money to the bottom line. That's where McKinsey wanted to have the greatest impact. It based its initial hypothesis—its definition of Allstate's problem—on a critical and unproven assumption: Allstate was overpaying legitimate claims.

How would McKinsey know that Allstate's problem was an overpayment of claims, which it also called *leakage*?[119] At this point, McKinsey hadn't seen a single Allstate claim file. The McKinsey slides provide no support for this critical assumption that Allstate was overpaying claims.

In a much later presentation called "The CCPR Quiz," after McKinsey conducted an extensive review of Allstate's claim files,

McKinsey asks this true-or-false question. "Over the past five years, [Allstate's] claim expense ratios and severity have increased significantly. Answer: False."

Based on its unproven assumption that Allstate was overpaying claims, however, McKinsey's solution—and the purpose of CCPR—was to drastically reduce Allstate's claims payments while maintaining Allstate's historically high premiums. Naturally, McKinsey never mentioned "the elephant in the room" during its presentation: the impending Sears IPO.

Allstate executives have been asked to explain how McKinsey could hypothesize that Allstate was overpaying claims when making this initial presentation. They respond: McKinsey's overpayment hypothesis was a subjective judgment by the McKinsey consultants who reviewed Allstate's claim files during the Closed File Survey. Unfortunately, this can't be true. This was McKinsey's *initial* presentation. McKinsey hadn't yet seen a single Allstate claim file.

One of the McKinsey slides sheds some light on this and provides a potential answer. "McKinsey Perspective on Claims," was another significant slide from the initial presentation.

McKinsey Perspective On Claims

1. The potential for economic improvement is substantial, *typically 5-15% reduction in severities and* 10-20% reduction in expenses

2. Identifying the nature of the opportunity is **not** the primary challenge; the primary barrier to improved performance is mobilizing a large organization to achieve significant improvement in front-line execution

3. In our experience, some companies make only modest progress against the economic opportunity, while others fully close the performance gap

4. Those companies that do push to eliminate economic leakage in Claims have the following characteristics:

   a) The senior management team views the improvement program as *a top priority*, with unanimity in their belief that change needs to occur

   b) They are willing to make *fundamental changes in* people, *procedures, management systems*, structure, etc.--to "*do whatever it takes*" and to attack organizational "sacred cows"

   c) They stick with it for several years until a changed culture is put in place

   d) They focus extraordinary attention on communication throughout the organization and throughout the process.

   e) They *invest significant time in measuring their performance*[120]

McKinsey's own perspective on claims demonstrates its pre-conceived ideas about claims transactions coming into the Allstate engagement. When McKinsey said Allstate's problem was overpaying legitimate claims, McKinsey based that statement on their assumption that *every* insurer overpaid claims. Therefore, every casualty insurer, including Allstate, should be able to immediately boost profits and shareholder value by reducing *all* claim payments by 5% to 15%—regardless of the individual merits of the claims.

The key issue for McKinsey was not *whether* Allstate was overpaying claims, but by *how much*. How fast could Allstate boost its profits by reducing claim payments—and get away with it? McKinsey was confident Allstate could make an immediate 5% to 15% reduction in claim payouts without too much grief from unsuspecting policyholders or ambivalent regulators.

McKinsey's Plan for Allstate

McKinsey's confidence in their solution was high, based on what they learned from their prior experience in the insurance industry.

- First, McKinsey knew Allstate wouldn't have to worry much about policyholders. Only a small fraction of All-state's policyholders would ever come face-to-face with its new claim-handling tactics. The vast majority would rely on Allstate's carefully crafted illusion of trust and protection built up over the years. While Allstate might lose a few policyholders because of its claims tactics, most policyholders would continue to pay higher-than-average premiums with little question.

- Second, McKinsey knew that roughly 80% of the tens of billions Allstate paid each year for claims involved small to mid-sized claims—worth between $1,500 to $15,000. The real savings wouldn't come from making large reductions on a few big claims. The big claims only totaled maybe $40 or $50 million a year.

The greatest savings—and increased profits—would come from forcing *millions* of claimants to accept $3,000 to $4,000 less for claims worth between $8,000 to $12,000. McKinsey correctly projected that, due to the vast numbers of these claims, the savings would add up to billions in extra profits for Allstate and its shareholders.

- Third, McKinsey wasn't worried about insurance regulators catching on. McKinsey already knew everything about the system regulators use to investigate insurance claim practices. In 1974, McKinsey invented the investigation system, the Market Conduct Examination, which the National Association of Insurance Commissioners (NAIC) adopted and has used in every state since then.[121] McKinsey knew exactly how to create improper profits without leaving any sign that a state insurance commissioner would act upon.

McKinsey knew its business model would only work if Allstate's senior executives aggressively pushed changes from the top down—and stuck with it for years. McKinsey told Allstate's executives that doing "whatever it takes" to reduce claim payments would mean sacrificing institutional "sacred cows." In light of its later statements about "radically altering" Allstate's whole approach to "the business of claims," the "sacred cows" McKinsey most likely referred to here were the traditional insurance rules requiring both prompt and fair payment of claims.[122] The underlying message was clear—adhering to the traditional rules would get in the way of McKinsey's solution to Allstate's "problem." This problem was Allstate's need to rapidly increase its profits and stock values.[123]

Changing Employee Behavior

Another key issue for McKinsey was whether Allstate's employees would go along with a system which underpaid legitimate claims. Allstate claims adjusters are ordinary people trying to make a living. Like most people in the workplace, they try to find out what management wants from them, and then act in ways that get them ahead in both salary and job security.

Most Allstate claims employees truly believe they're providing good service to the policyholders, the public, and the company. For years, Allstate trained these employees to follow traditional insurance rules. How would McKinsey convince these claim handlers to follow a new set of rules?

In its "Perspective on Claims CPR" slide, McKinsey explains how it intended to induce the Allstate employee to accept its system of underpaying claims for profit. Allstate should use annual employee performance measures—like the performance measures McKinsey instituted at Enron.

These measures would be critical to both employee acceptance and the ultimate success of CCPR. The performance measures really came down to one thing. Did the employee's performance, whether at the bottom or the top of the company, contribute to increased profits and shareholder value? If so, Allstate would advance and reward those employees. If not, those employees' jobs with Allstate would be in jeopardy.

McKinsey Perspective On Claims CPR

1. Examination of the appropriateness of expense levels necessitates understanding the impact on severities.

2. Determining the economic trade-offs between expenses and severities must be done factually at the claim handling transaction level.

3. Litigation management is a critical skill with significant impact on a carrier's overall performance.

4. Against a standard of "best practices," claim handling and litigation management execution gaps are typically substantial.

* * *

7. *Measurement systems that track claim performance in economic terms are critical to successful implementation.*

8. The claim function needs to be led from a general management perspective.[124]

Changing the Claims Organization at Allstate

McKinsey's initial presentation in September 1992 also provides a fairly complete overview of McKinsey's three-part solution for redesigning Allstate's claim factory.

- First, McKinsey would set the machinery at Allstate's claim factory to under-fill every can of Allstate insurance by at least 5% to 15%, while still charging the same, or even higher, prices for each can. McKinsey would set the factory machinery to do this by installing a computer program called Colossus, discussed more fully in Chapter 12, "Colossus," starting on page 119.

- Second, McKinsey would encourage employees to accept the new program through performance measurements and incentives. These incentives reward and advance only those employees who meet or exceed Allstate's measurements.

- Third, McKinsey would use Allstate's financial superiority over policyholders to withhold its product (claim payments) from its paying customers when they need it most: at the time of a loss. Customers could only get their money when they agreed to accept less than what they paid for.

McKinsey's first "Key Principle" of CCPR was that it "ignores existing organizational or functional boundaries." This was also the first teaching of McKinsey's business model at Enron—encouraging senior executives to find creative ways to ignore boundaries and "think outside the box."

By ignoring the existing ethical boundaries of the insurance industry, McKinsey was asking Allstate to do more than just think outside the *box*. It was telling Allstate to think outside the *rules*—in much the same way Enron's senior management was doing under McKinsey's guidance, with spectacular results.

Allstate's senior executives accepted McKinsey's idea of thinking outside the rules. They posed no obstacle to McKinsey's claim system dedicated to making the shareholders' interest Allstate's top priority. Placing shareholders' interests ahead of the public's and ahead of Allstate's policyholders made a lot of sense to management. However, every executive at that meeting should have also known that it made the company's promise of protection to policyholders a lie.

McKinsey designed its claim system around the zero-sum game approach to business ethics which Gordon Gekko endorsed six years earlier in *Wall Street*.

8

The Zero-sum Game

Policyholders versus Shareholders

I N ONE of the most important McKinsey slides, McKinsey lays out its mission statement for redesigning claim handling at Allstate—and for the entire insurance industry. According to McKinsey, it's "change goal" was to "redefine the game... to radically alter our whole approach to the business of claims."[125] For McKinsey, redefining the game meant replacing the traditional rules of insurance with its zero-sum game business model. Radically altering Allstate's whole approach to the business of insurance would mean creating a business model at Allstate that committed every employee and resource to a single goal—"doing whatever it takes" in an amoral, relentless pursuit of profits.

McKinsey's Game

In designing Allstate's claim system, McKinsey turned this single goal into the most important measure of employee performance. It would also become the only legitimate concern for Allstate's senior management. This is why Allstate adopted stock ownership goals for its senior executives in 1996, and why it tells its shareholders today that "we believe strongly in linking the interests of management with those of our shareholders."

This pursuit of profit is also why Allstate's response to its record profits over the past two years has been over 650 price increases—despite its competitors' reduced premiums in response to similar record profits. It also explains Allstate's lack of concern for its policyholders in the devastated Gulf region. It explains why, as reported in the *New York Times,* Allstate's claim tactics are forcing thousands of unnecessary lawsuits, and slowing recovery in the Gulf region for what will likely be many years to come.[126]

The McKinsey slides also show that McKinsey applied its business model to *all* claims Allstate handled—including homeowner and catastrophe claims. In a July 1995 McKinsey slide entitled "Allstate Personal Lines—CCPR Benefit Projections," McKinsey projected that applying CCPR's model to homeowners claims would reduce Allstate's homeowner claim payments by as much as $400 million between 1996 and 1999.[127]

After McKinsey's intervention, the game of insurance at Allstate would no longer be about the best interests of its policyholders. The game would be about a never-ending quest for profit.

"Zero-sum economic game" are the words McKinsey used in another of the most defining McKinsey slides, shown on the next page. This slide describes how its new claim handling system at Allstate would work—and is still working today in every claim Allstate handles.

Improving Allstate's casualty economics will have a *negative economic impact on some medical providers, plaintiff attorneys, and claimants.*

CASUALTY OPPORTUNITY IDENTIFICATION

Dollars

Zero Sum Economic Game
--*Allstate Gains*
--*Others must lose*

Powerful opponents
--plaintiffs' bar

| Fair Value | Abusive Medical Testing/ Treatment | Unnecessary Plaintiff Attorney Payments | Claimant Payments Above Fair Value[127] | Current Payments |

83

McKinsey's new approach at Allstate did more than radically alter the traditional rules governing insurance. It obliterated them. It created a direct competition between Allstate's shareholders and its policyholders. Such a competition is directly contrary to the public purpose behind insurance, and the special responsibilities insurers owe to their policyholders and the public.

The following statement about an insurer's responsibilities comes from the California Supreme Court in 1979. Scholars and courts alike almost universally accept this as the definitive statement of what the law has been over the past 100 years.

> The insurer's obligations are . . . rooted in their status as purveyors of a vital service labeled quasi-public in nature. Suppliers of services affected with a public interest must take the public's interest seriously, where necessary placing it *before their interest in maximizing gains and limiting disbursements.*[128]

This famous statement describes the important difference between how insurers must operate and how ordinary businesses operate. It also explains why McKinsey's use of the zero-sum game as its business model for claim handling at Allstate isn't just inappropriate—it's a direct violation of the traditional rules of insurance.

McKinsey's idea for redesigning Allstate's business systems wasn't new. It was based on principles that had proven successful for many ordinary businesses. However, McKinsey forgot, or deliberately ignored, one critical fact. An insurance company like Allstate is *not* an ordinary business. Allstate cannot operate under the same principles as an ordinary business—no matter how successful those principles have been.

As the California Supreme Court explains, insurers must operate under a different set of principles. The states license them to provide a "vital public service." In accepting the *privilege* to operate an insurance company, insurers agree to abide by the rules that come along with a business "affected with a public interest." These are the responsibilities and rules McKinsey advised Allstate to ignore.

As we've seen in Chapter 2, about 70% of all the money an insurer collects in premiums is money the insurer should hold in trust for its policyholders to pay their legitimate claims. That claims money is like a trust fund. The money in the claims fund belongs to the policyholders. It does *not* belong to Allstate. It certainly does not belong to Allstate's shareholders or executives.

As also stated, the insurer holds its policyholders' claim money "on deposit," like a bank, under a promise the insurer will use that money to pay all the legitimate claims of its policyholders. If the insurer is doing its job honestly, and charging a fair premium, there should be little, if any, of that claim money left over to go to the company and its shareholders as excess operating profit. Insurers also shouldn't have to save any leftover claim money for a future natural disaster. That's the purpose for the company's surplus.

There shouldn't be any claim money left over, because the insurer already builds its profit into the premiums it charges. Any insurer who uses the claim process to take extra operating profits from the policyholder's claim fund is not doing its job honestly or charging a fair premium. It is shortchanging its policyholders and violating the public trust under which it is licensed to operate.

In using its zero-sum game business model at Allstate, McKinsey also forgot or ignored two other important differences between insurers and ordinary businesses. First, policyholders are not like the customers of an ordinary business. Policyholders have a direct financial interest in how the insurer runs its business—a financial interest that is *greater* than the interest of the insurer's shareholders in maximizing profits. It's the policyholders' money the insurer uses to pay claims—to provide the public service for which it is licensed.

Second, paying legitimate claims fairly and promptly must be *the* primary purpose of every insurer licensed to operate. Boosting profits and shareholder values may be important to the private interests of the company and its shareholders. However, as the California Supreme Court has stated, an insurer's public license means these private interests must come second. The first interest is the policyholders (and the public's) in having legitimate claims paid fairly and promptly.

Both Allstate and McKinsey knew when they designed CCPR, that using a zero-sum game business model would be improper, and could expose Allstate to claims of insurance bad faith. That's why another important McKinsey slide, entitled "Wining the Economic Game—Changing the Rules," recommends that Allstate become an "industry leader" in "modifying the bad faith laws."

WINNING THE ECONOMIC GAME:

CHANGING THE RULES

Objective
Shift advantage away from claimants and
plaintiff attorneys

Criteria
Requires *targeted changes in public policy*
New *Allstate industry leadership role*

Potential examples
Targeted *tort reform*
Modify bad faith laws
Mandated health providers
Improved procedural rules (e.g. discovery)

NEW GAME

Objective
Build...competitive advantage through
fundamental rethinking of industry and our
approach

Criteria
--*Radically different* processes and
  organization
--*Redefinition of claims benefits* and
  payment approach
--Application of leading edge
  technologies...[129]

Here, McKinsey is advising Allstate to become a leader in "changing the rules" because McKinsey knew the bad faith laws in every state prohibited insurers from doing exactly what CCPR was designed to do. If there was nothing wrong with using McKinsey's business model, then McKinsey would have had no reason to advise Allstate to "modify… the bad faith laws."

Until April, 2008, few people in America have seen the McKinsey slides and judged for themselves whether Allstate's approach to paying claims is right or wrong. Until very recently, Allstate successfully kept the public and lawmakers ignorant about its business model.

Tort Reform and the Zero-sum Game

As the "Winning the Economic Game" slide on page 87 states, targeted tort reform would also play an important role in changing the rules and winning McKinsey's zero-sum economic game. But how would tort reform help Allstate (and other insurers) win? As with all things McKinsey, there's only one answer: because it boosts insurer profits. However, just how would tort reform help Allstate boost profits?

Carefully targeted media campaigns (driven primarily by the insurance industry) have conditioned most people to believe that tort reform is a good thing. The popular belief is that tort reform means putting a stop to the supposedly countless frivolous lawsuits which greedy plaintiffs file every day. Unscrupulous trial lawyers represent these plaintiffs, and get rich with these suits.

The poster child of the tort reform debate is the now-legendary 1994 McDonald's coffee case—where a jury awarded $2.86 million to a woman who burned herself with hot coffee.[130] Although the verdict was later reduced by the judge to $640,000, this case became a flashpoint in the national debate over the both the need for tort reform and the number of truly frivolous lawsuits actually being filed.[131]

That debate, and the belief that millions of frivolous lawsuits are being filed every year, still persist. On May 2, 2007, ABC News' Law & Justice Unit aired a Special Report entitled "I'm Being Sued for WHAT?"[132] In this program, ABC News reported that, according to the National Federation of Independent Business, "[t]ort claims cost the country hundreds of billions of dollars per year."[133]

Tort claims are the kind of claims that casualty insurance companies pay. The casualty insurance industry issues billions of dollars in coverage to the businesses which special interest groups like the National Federation of Independent Business and the National Chamber of Commerce represent. If these statements about tort claims were true, then we should also expect to see the casualty insurance industry as a whole paying "hundreds of billions of dollars" each year for frivolous casualty claims—and suffering major losses.

Yet, on April 18, 2007 (just two weeks before ABC News aired its report), the National Underwriter Property & Casualty, an insurance industry group, reported a very different story about how the casualty insurance industry was doing financially.[134] The headline of its magazine article (published April 23, 2007) read "P-C Insurers Post Record Combined Ratio, As Net Income Skyrockets To $64 Billion—Industry braces to defend against accusations of gouging consumers on price."[135]

In comparing the industry's record profits in 2006 to those of 2005, the article contains a statistical insert entitled "Big Bucks." The Big Bucks analysis shows that while earned casualty premiums increased by $18 billion from 2005 to 2006, pre-tax operating income for the industry as a whole jumped from $45.1 billion in 2005 to $84.6 billion in 2006—an increase of $40 billion.

Quoting Michael Murray, Vice President of Insurance Services Office, Inc.,[136] National Underwriter attributed the casualty insurance industry's record profits in 2006 to a "Goldilocks" convergence of four factors.

1. State tort reform laws.

2. Federal class-action reform laws.

3. Fewer reported auto claims.

4. Lower-than-expected payment of claims which had been pending from the years 1997-2001 (presumably due to litigation) allowing the addition of $6 billion in profits from money the industry had previously designated as "reserves" to pay those claims.[137]

The subject of this book is how McKinsey's claim tactics are affecting policyholders and claimants—this is not a book specifically about tort reform. However the steady drumbeat of calls for more tort reform, and widespread claims of frivolous lawsuits like those reported as fact by ABC News show that McKinsey's public-relations strategy is effective. With the casualty insurance industry enjoying skyrocketing profits, it hardly seems like an appropriate time to change the rules through tort reform and win its zero-sum economics game.

In retrospect, McKinsey could arguably be credited as the author of the current mythology surrounding casualty insurance claims and the people who make those claims. Popular mythology holds that the vast majority of casualty insurance claims and lawsuits are frivolous and most people who make casualty claims or file lawsuits for benefits are just trying to win the lawsuit lottery.[138]

Thanks to these McKinsey-inspired public relations campaigns, this is what most people believe today about people who make claims or file lawsuits to get those claims fairly paid. Part of the reason for this popular myth is that most of us have never had to make a serious insurance claim. We've never been forced to file a lawsuit just to get our claims fairly paid. Those who have had this experience know better.

One of the goals of this book is to help consumers see through these popular myths. What we really need isn't tort reform—it's insurance reform. Certainly, *some* people, and *some* lawyers, file ridiculous lawsuits. There are indeed more lawsuits being filed today.

However, the *real* frivolous lawsuits—the ones costing taxpayers billions of dollars every year—are the ones which insurers following McKinsey's business model force on their own policyholders. The insurers' primary goal is to dramatically increase profits—regardless of whether that means broken promises for policyholders. These insurers are not competing with each other; they're competing with their own customers. One need look no further than the industry's present skyrocketing profits to see how successful McKinsey's followers have been.

9

Good Hands or
Boxing Gloves

The Zero-sum Game
Against Policyholders

T HE TITLE of this book, *From Good Hands to Boxing Gloves,* isn't my invention. It's a direct quote from what may be the most dramatic—and damning—of all the McKinsey slides.

After subjectively confirming its "initial hypothesis" that All-state was overpaying claims, McKinsey set out to design, test, and implement its solution. McKinsey's solution is what I like to call the *Fair or Prompt—But Not Both* formula for paying claims. McKinsey designed the fair or prompt payment plan to exploit Allstate's two biggest advantages in the claims process. Their first advantage is the policyholder's financial vulnerability to delay, and the second is Allstate's overwhelming experience and resources when litigating over claim values. Here is what McKinsey's February 16, 1994, "Good Hands or Boxing Gloves" slide looks like.

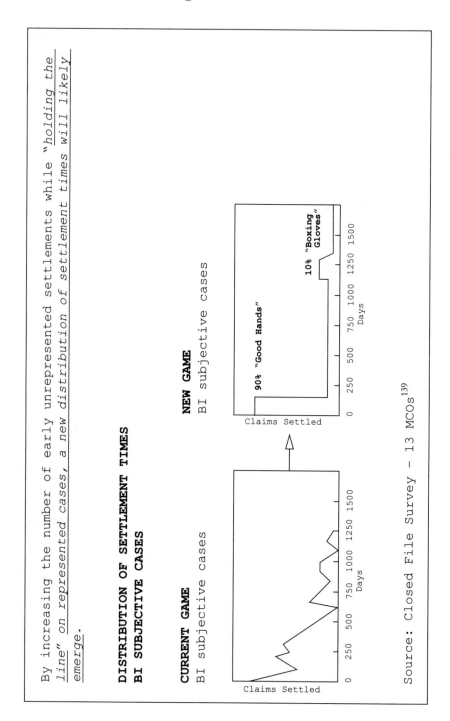

By increasing the number of early unrepresented settlements while *"holding the line"* on represented cases, a new distribution of settlement times *will likely emerge*.

DISTRIBUTION OF SETTLEMENT TIMES
BI SUBJECTIVE CASES

CURRENT GAME

BI subjective cases

NEW GAME

BI subjective cases

Claims Settled

0   250   500   750   1000   1250   1500
Days

Claims Settled

90% "Good Hands"

10% "Boxing Gloves"

0   250   500   750   1000   1250   1500
Days

Source: Closed File Survey – 13 MCOs[139]

This slide explains how McKinsey intended to exploit Allstate's financial advantages over policyholders. Under the "Current Game" graph, Allstate paid claims based on their individual merits, without using delay as a settlement tactic. As a result, they settled all claims after about 1,250 days (about three and a half years), with lots of peaks and valleys in settlements between day one and day 1,250. However, Allstate's current process did not produce the dramatic increase in profits McKinsey projected as possible in its Initial Presentation of September 27, 1992.[140]

Under the "New Game" graph, Allstate would settle about 90% of all claims within the first 180 days after the loss. These claimants would get Allstate's "Good Hands" treatment. The remaining 10% of the claims would take about four years or more to settle. These claimants would get Allstate's "boxing gloves" treatment.

Here's what the terms *good hands* and *boxing gloves* as used in this slide really mean. From its experience in the insurance industry, McKinsey knew several important facts about the claims process.

- First, about 80% of all the billions of dollars Allstate paid out were for claims worth between $1,500 and $15,000—small to mid-sized claims. Reducing claims payments for these all-important small to mid-sized claims, even if only by a few thousand dollars per claim, would add up to billions in profits.

- Second, McKinsey also knew that claim payments to policyholders with an attorney averaged about five times more than claim payments to policyholders without an attorney.[141] So, keeping policyholders away from attorneys as long as possible—especially the policyholders with small to mid-sized claims—would be very important.

- Third, the most important thing McKinsey knew was how critical Allstate's approach to policyholders during the first 90 to 180 days after a loss would be to reducing claim payments. McKinsey understood the importance of delaying payment: Allstate could earn additional interest on the claimant's money, *and* this critical time is when most claimants would really begin to feel the financial pressures of the loss. Claimants would be at their most vulnerable to the kind of pressure McKinsey intended to apply.

Consequently, McKinsey designed CCPR to keep policyholders waiting and away from attorneys during this critical period. The policyholders would get false assurances that they didn't need an attorney, because Allstate would be making a "fair" offer "soon" to settle their claim. McKinsey knew this approach would convince most policyholders to just wait for Allstate's fair offer—and keep away from attorneys. What Allstate didn't tell policyholders is that their fair offer would not appear for 90 to 180 days.

Keeping policyholders waiting, away from attorneys, with promises of forthcoming fair offers, would provide Allstate with its best opportunity to exploit the policyholder's financial vulnerability from the loss. This formed the foundation for McKinsey's "Good Hands or Boxing Gloves" strategy.

McKinsey created scripts for Allstate's adjusters to read to policyholders throughout these first 180 days. McKinsey intended the scripts to build empathy in order to keep policyholders waiting and away from attorneys. Allstate trained and monitored their adjustors on using these scripts, which had a "good news—bad news" model.

The good news in the scripts was the message that Allstate really cared about the policyholder and was honestly trying to help the policyholder get the claim settled as soon as possible. The adjustor would gradually give the policyholder the bad news that Allstate needed more information and more time before they could make an offer. Days stretched into weeks, weeks into months— until finally the policyholder really felt the financial pressure of the loss. Right on target, at 90 to 180 days.

This would be the critical point—the moment Allstate would spring the trap. The policyholder, at his or her most financially vulnerable point, would get the *really* bad news—Allstate's lowball claim offer for about 60% of the real value of the claim.

McKinsey's "New Game" graph on page 94 shows 90% of claims settling within the first 180 days. This is because McKinsey knew that 90% of the claimants would give in. The mounting financial pressures of the loss, combined with the realization that fighting Allstate in court wouldn't make any financial sense, would make a low offer look good. As the old saying goes, a bird in the hand is worth two in the bush.

The 90% of policyholders who accepted about 60¢ on the dollar for their claims are the only ones who would get "Good Hands" treatment (if we can call forcing a substantial reduction in the benefits "Good Hands" treatment). These policyholders would get prompt payment under McKinsey's plan.

If the policyholder wouldn't accept Allstate's "Good Hands" offer, then McKinsey's plan called for Allstate to aggressively investigate the claim. This investigation was an excuse to delay and withhold all payment unless the policyholder either gave in or finally forced Allstate to pay after years of costly, bitter, no-compromise litigation.

Litigation would be the only way a policyholder could get fair payment under McKinsey's zero-sum game. As this slide shows, McKinsey planned this process so that it would take years, in some cases more than five years, for these policyholders to get their claims paid fairly. The intended result of McKinsey's zero-sum game was to present the policyholder with only two choices: prompt payment *or* fair payment—but not both. This is what McKinsey meant by "90% Good Hands" and "10% Boxing Gloves."

A few policyholders might eventually win a "boxing gloves" fight with Allstate. But fair payment would come at such a terrible price in terms of delay and expense that winning would be a Pyrrhic victory for the policyholder: so costly it wasn't worth winning.[142] McKinsey's "boxing gloves" tactic would also serve as a warning to deter other policyholders from refusing Allstate's first offers in the future. McKinsey estimated that only about 10% of policyholders would be able to go the distance in a fifteen-round fight against a trained professional like Allstate.

This McKinsey slide may be the smoking-gun evidence of Allstate's intent to violate the traditional rules of insurance. Of course, Allstate knew that traditional insurance laws expressly forbade McKinsey's "Good Hands or Boxing Gloves" approach. Traditional rules required Allstate to pay all legitimate claims fairly *and* promptly. This was why McKinsey needed to convince Allstate's senior executives that they should "think outside the rules" when designing its new claim handling system.

Traditional insurance rules require the insurer to give *equal* consideration to the policyholder's interest during the claim handling process. McKinsey's business model makes Allstate's policyholders its competitors. Equal consideration of the competitor is impossible in a zero-sum game. The object is to take as much as possible away from the competitors. McKinsey's model places the interests of Allstate's shareholders above the interests of its policyholders.

This also leads to McKinsey's other fundamental departure from the traditional insurance rules. In a zero-sum game, the only relevant distinctions between claimants are those that tend to reduce claim payments and increase profits. Consequently, McKinsey designed CCPR to treat the interests of Allstate's premium-paying policyholders exactly the same as if they were third-party strangers to the insurance contract.

First- and Third-party Claims

Under traditional insurance laws, the policyholder is the paying customer who bought the insurance. The policyholder has a contractual relationship with the insurer. If the policyholder, for instance, is injured by an uninsured driver or has a fire in his house, the policyholder makes a claim with his insurer. This is called a *first-party* claim—the person who bought the insurance makes the claim. These types of claims are not supposed to be adversarial. Back to our banking analogy in Chapter 3—according to the fiduciary principle, the insurer is supposed to give equal or greater weight to the policyholder's needs than to their own financial motives.

The policy also covers any person the policyholder accidentally injures or any property the policyholder accidentally damages. People whom the policyholder injures or damages are called *third-party claimants*, because they are not one of the two parties to the insurance contract. The insurer pays the claims which the third-party claimants make. However, the insurer has no contractual relationship with those claimants.

In theory, the insurer's first loyalty is always to the policyholder. The insurer must make reasonable efforts to make the third-party claimants whole again so they do not need to resort to legal action against the policyholder. The insurer's duty is to prevent undue stress or hardship for the policyholder by taking care of anyone the policyholder accidentally injures. When third parties sue, they put the policyholder's name on the complaint—not the insurer's. For reasons that seem silly these days, courts still cling to the outdated idea that the jury will award more money if it knows that the defendant has insurance.

However, McKinsey's procedures for handling policyholders' claims are exactly the same as those for handling claims of third-party strangers.[143] This is only logical under a zero-sum game business model. Whether policyholders are themselves claimants, or are the ones against whom a third party makes a claim, the policyholder's interests are always in conflict with McKinsey's objective. That objective is increasing profits by taking money away from the policyholders' claim fund.

In other words, Allstate gains—policyholders and claimants must lose. This happens because, as the McKinsey slides state, a "key part" of McKinsey's strategy was to provoke "significantly higher levels of litigation" with anyone who refused to accept Allstate's "Good Hands" offers.[144]

Litigation as a Tool

No doubt, McKinsey saw how effective aggressive litigation tactics could be as a tool for reducing claim payments during its State Farm engagement. McKinsey knew from its experience at State Farm that Allstate would have a big advantage over plaintiffs in the litigation process. Allstate had this advantage whether the plaintiffs were Allstate policyholders trying to get fair payment, or third parties forced to sue Allstate's policyholders because of Allstate's refusal to make fair offers.

In addition, Allstate does not *aggressively use litigation to maintain fair settlement values* in the market

[Pie chart showing 75% of cases are represented with side bar graph showing 55% with no case filed, 41% filed a case, only 4% of 517 represented cases went to verdict]

Plaintiff Attorney quotes:

"State Farm *is terrible to deal with*; they are not afraid to go to trial"

"State Farm has driven values down in this market by going to court and winning some cases"

"State Farm has a *clear strategy to drive down market values through going to trial*...I don't like it and it will hurt them in the long run."

Source: Closed File Survey—13 MCOs, team analysis[145]

The reality is that Allstate, like State Farm, simply has more money and more experience in litigation than most plaintiffs or their attorneys. McKinsey also knew Allstate would have another important ally in litigation—time.

Delaying payment does two things:

- Benefits the insurer, which is earning investment income while it holds the policyholder's money.

- Hurts the claimant, who needs that money to replace his or her loss.

An article in *Risk Management Magazine* explains how insurers use delay to their advantage.

> When an insurance company denies a claim, most policyholders simply give up. Insurance companies win by default. Delay works in favor of insurance companies. Insurance handling and insurance coverage litigation…have four speeds: slow, very slow, stop, and reverse…Thus, *the entire litigation system— its enormous costs and lengthy delays—works to the advantage of the insurance company.*[146]

It clearly made no difference to Allstate that deliberately forcing "significantly higher levels of litigation" *against its own policyholders* was not giving equal consideration to its policyholders' interests. It also made no difference to McKinsey, or to Allstate, that forcing increased levels of litigation would necessarily inflict damage on those policyholders.

The article in *Risk Management Magazine* also explains how insurers have a second incentive to delay claims: the time-value of the money they hold in trust.

> The system is structured so that the insurance company, by denying a claim, gains the time-value of the money and the likelihood that the claim will be settled for less than its full value. Moreover, at the

same time the policyholder is fighting an uphill battle against the insurance company's lawyers, it is
forced to defend endless allegations of fraud by the
claims adjuster. Whether in negotiation or in litigation, the insurance companies win by saying
"NO."[147]

Being named as a defendant in a civil suit inflicts financial and
emotional costs that the policyholder bought insurance to avoid. A
lawsuit is a public record. While the suit is pending, the policyholder must disclose it as a potential financial liability. A judgment
is enforceable for many years. Even if Allstate eventually pays the
judgment, it may not happen for years due to lengthy appeals and
post-judgment motions. Meanwhile, a monetary judgment, especially one in excess of policy limits, can pose significant credit
problems for the policyholder caught in the middle.

Aggressive investigation and litigation tactics are essential components of McKinsey's zero-sum game. However, such aggression
from Allstate can provoke similar aggression from plaintiffs' attorneys. Again, the policyholders pay the price. The policyholders
must endure frequent and invasive interrogatories about their private lives, longer and more hostile depositions, and uncomfortable,
if not embarrassing, cross-examinations at trial. Then they have the
natural distress of being put on trial for their actions in a public
forum, especially in a small community.

When buying an Allstate policy, people believe they are buying
security from loss and peace of mind. Allstate's advertising leads
them to believe they will be in "Good Hands." They would never
buy Allstate insurance if they knew Allstate intended to give them
"boxing gloves" treatment should they ever try to obtain the benefit of their policies. They also would never buy Allstate insurance if
they knew they were signing up to be pawns in Allstate's battle plan
to win McKinsey's game. A statement from a case, *Campbell v. State
Farm Mutual Insurance Company*, explains this idea.

> An allegation that one's negligent conduct has caused the injury or death of another inevitably triggers fear and apprehension that insurance succors. Insureds buy financial protection and peace of mind against fortuitous losses. *They pay the requisite premiums and put their faith and trust in their insurers to pay policy benefits promptly and fairly when the insured event occurs.* Good faith and fair dealing is their expectation. It is the very essence of the insurer-insured relationship. In some instances, however, insurance companies refuse to pay the promised benefits when the underwritten harm occurs. When an insurer decides to delay or to deny paying benefits, the policyholder can suffer injury not only to his economic well-being but to his emotional and physical health as well. Moreover, the holder of a policy with low monetary limits may see his whole claim virtually wiped out by expenses if the insurance company compels him to resort to court action.[148]

McKinsey's "Good Hands or Boxing Gloves" strategy does more than ignore the policyholder's interest in buying an Allstate policy. It actively defeats that interest. McKinsey designed this strategy to provoke the very anguish and distress policyholders were trying to avoid when they bought insurance in the first place: "a lot of vexatious, time-consuming, [and] expensive litigation."[149]

10

We Get What
We Measure

MCKINSEY KNEW Allstate could not win its zero-sum game unless its employees were making the right plays. In McKinsey's own words, "Current processes are incenting and reinforcing behavior that *does not reward shareholders.*"[150]

Traditional Insurance Rules at Allstate

McKinsey was complaining about Allstate's employees following traditional insurance rules. By doing so, McKinsey believed Allstate's employees were rewarding policyholders instead of shareholders. That didn't fit with McKinsey's business model.

The "current processes" that were not "rewarding shareholders" were traditional measures of claims department performance. These traditional measures tracked how promptly and economically the staff investigated and resolved claims. Under the traditional rules, the insurer relied on the experience and independent judgment of its local adjusters to evaluate each claim according to its individual merits. Adjusters used negotiating tactics to invite compromise on both sides in order to arrive at a fair value.

105

McKinsey knew the best way to convince employees to accept its program was through performance measurements. Employees naturally respond to whatever the company measures regarding their performance. To enforce change, McKinsey needed a new set of performance measures geared to its business model instead of traditional insurance rules.

As McKinsey put it: "We get what we measure. Currently we measure expenses and pending [the traditional insurance rules]. The new measurement approach will be based on the processes and activities required to achieve the *desired outcomes* [increasing profits]."[151]

In order for CCPR to produce higher profits, McKinsey needed to persuade Allstate's employees that underpaying claims was more important than "employee satisfaction, file quality, or customer satisfaction." We've already seen McKinsey's business model at work in Allstate's executive compensation plan and the lottery-like fortunes it produced for Allstate's top executives. McKinsey would apply this same business model—with far more modest rewards—to Allstate's frontline employees to motivate them to make claim decisions that reward Allstate's shareholders.

Allstate's Employee Incentive Programs

The affidavit of former Allstate frontline adjuster, Shannon Kmatz, reveals how pervasive and covert McKinsey's system of incentives and rewards is at Allstate. When starting employment, Allstate provided its local adjusters with a regional office document entitled "Regional Office Expense Policy." Allstate also provided a blue Allstate CitiBank credit card—which the adjusters affectionately referred to as "Big Blue."[152]

Allstate adjusters received rewards and incentives, mainly credits on their Allstate Big Blue credit cards, which they could spend freely. The incentives also included a variety of specific benefits, such as Beanie Babies, lunches, travel, movie tickets, postage stamps, coupons for merchandise, gift certificates, paid time off, and lottery tickets.[153]

Within a year after Allstate put CCPR into place, McKinsey discovered that CCPR was not achieving the expected reductions in loss payouts. The reason: too many employees still adhered to the traditional rules, as Allstate had trained them to do, instead of embracing McKinsey's new business model.[154]

Measuring Compliance with Colossus

As part of CCPR, McKinsey installed a company-wide computer system called Colossus, which assigned claim values. Colossus is a computer program that evaluates claim values after an adjuster puts in the accident information. McKinsey found that Allstate adjusters were not adhering to the Colossus computer values because they did not believe the values were fair. If an adjustor uses Colossus as Allstate intended, they do not actually adjust anything. Instead, they merely communicate the computer-generated values. We will discuss Colossus more fully in Chapter 12.

McKinsey established a "watchdog" in every claim office called an Evaluation Consultant. McKinsey then developed job-performance measurements for both the watchdog *and* the adjusters. The evaluation consultant's job was to review every Colossus evaluation generated by every adjuster in the office. The evaluation consultant checks every adjuster's Colossus input, and then sets a claim value for every claim called the Evaluated Amount. The Allstate adjuster communicates this non-negotiable, "Good Hands" offer to the claimant.

Colossus' reporting programs allow Allstate to track the evaluation consultant's job performance as well as each adjuster's job performance in the region on a monthly basis. Allstate measures the evaluation consultant's performance by comparing the final settlement amount to the Colossus evaluation. In turn, the evaluation consultant measures the adjuster's job performance by comparing the amount paid to the evaluated amount. Allstate called these measures *Evaluated to Colossus* for the evaluation consultant and *Paid to Evaluated Amount* for the adjuster.

Paid to Evaluated Amount would now become the ultimate—and indeed, the only—legitimate measure of performance from top to bottom at Allstate.[155] Paid to Evaluated Amount would also become the goal of every action that every employee takes on a claim, from the claims office to the courtroom.

In measuring the adjuster's job performance by comparing actual payments to the Colossus values, Allstate encouraged adjusters to convince policyholders to accept their prompt but unfair settlement offers. These new performance measures would force adjusters to see claimants who resisted their initial settlement offers as an obstacle to achieving good job performance evaluations. This would make it natural for adjusters to use McKinsey's "boxing gloves" approach in response to such resistance. In turn, this has created a corporate culture at Allstate that encourages claims employees to treat policyholders making claims as their adversaries.

These job-performance measures have their most profound impact on the adjuster's ability to negotiate claim values. Allstate strongly discourages compromise. Allstate grades adjusters on their take-it-or-leave-it negotiating techniques which prohibit reevaluating the computer-driven claim values.

As we've seen in Chapter 3, the traditional insurance rules prevent insurers from creating such a corporate culture. The reason is simple. Policyholders pay the premiums that pay not only their own legitimate claims, but also the salaries of *every* Allstate claims employee.[156] On the other hand, third-party strangers making claims against Allstate's policyholders do not pay premiums. In most cases, therefore, these third parties cannot expect to be treated like paying customers. They can legitimately be viewed as "adversaries" to both Allstate and its policyholders.[157]

The Supreme Court of Arizona gives an excellent description of what it means to be treated with equal consideration by your own insurance company.

> The carrier has an obligation to immediately conduct an adequate investigation, act reasonably in evaluating the claim, and act promptly in paying a legitimate claim. It should do nothing that jeopardizes the insured's security under the policy. *It should not force an insured to go through needless adversarial hoops to achieve its rights under the policy. It cannot lowball claims or delay claims hoping that the insured will settle for less.* Equal consideration of the insured requires more than that.[158]

As we'll see in the next chapter, forcing insureds through needless adversarial hoops is exactly how McKinsey designed Allstate's litigation system to work. One McKinsey slide says a "major component" of CCPR's "negotiation/settlement" strategy is to "stand firm on final offer with no real negotiation... [and] avoid [the] trap of courthouse step settlements." Under CCPR, compromise would no longer play a role in settling claims. Allstate designed this strategy to drive policyholders headlong into the "kill box" of McKinsey's zero-sum game plan—the American civil justice system.[159]

11

Stepping Into the Ring

Fighting Against Allstate's Boxing Gloves

H AVE YOU ever been involved in a divorce or in custody proceedings? Have you ever visited a doctor for a medical concern that you wanted to keep private? Have you ever had a less than stellar review at work? We will see in this chapter how Allstate uses private and sometimes embarrassing information as fair game in litigation for insurance claims.

As we saw in the previous chapter, McKinsey designed CCPR to substantially increase the number of policyholder lawsuits by preventing any real negotiation over its computer-generated claim values. At the end of the last chapter, I called the American civil justice system the "kill box" of McKinsey's CCPR program.[159] This is because under McKinsey's litigation plan, going to court against Allstate to get fair payment can feel like being caught in an ambush.

How a Lawsuit Works

Most people have never filed a claim during the McKinsey era at Allstate. Most of us have no idea what this really means.

Part One: Discovery

The first part of Allstate's litigation plan involves what's called discovery. Discovery is the set of court procedures established for gathering information from the other side needed to prove or disprove facts that could determine how the judge or jury might decide the issues in the case. Discovery procedures usually involve several methods of gathering information.

- *Interrogatories* are written questions to the other side.

- *Depositions* are in-person questioning sessions between the claimant and the attorneys, and sometimes a consultant or specialist.

- *Requests for production* are written requests to the other side for copies of documents.

- *Subpoenas* are court orders commanding people or companies who are not involved in the case to produce certain documents

Under McKinsey's game plan, Allstate uses discovery not just to gather information important to the claim. They use it to pry as far as possible into irrelevant—and sometimes embarrassing—details of the policyholder's life. Then they disseminate that information to embarrass the policyholder and weaken their case.

Allstate lawyers typically ask policyholders to produce their personal medical records for their *entire* lifetime, no matter when the injury occurred. Allstate lawyers also serve subpoenas on *every* doctor or hospital they even suspect has treated the policyholder for *any* reason—including a policyholder's gynecological or psychiatric records. Some Allstate attorneys routinely issue subpoenas for a policyholder's medical records to every doctor and hospital in the town where the policyholder lives, or has ever lived.

This can be quite intimidating—and in a small town, quite embarrassing. In addition, Allstate lawyers also routinely demand that policyholders be examined by doctors known to issue medical opinions that are favorable to Allstate.

Allstate lawyers don't stop at medical records. They also typically subpoena a policyholder's tax returns, financial records, and bank records for the past ten years—even when the policyholder is not making a claim for lost income. Employment records are another favorite target. Subpoenas for personnel files are regularly served on every known employer of the policyholder—again, even if no claim for loss of employment is being made. Allstate then combs the employment records for reprimands, demotions, denials of raises, firings, or any negative information about the policyholder—even if it has nothing to do with the claim.

Another standard practice is searching public records and databases for any negative information on the policyholder. These include lifetime searches for arrest records, including traffic citations. They also search for mortgage and lien information, prior insurance claims of any kind, and any kind of lawsuit where the policyholder's name appears—including records of divorce proceedings and custody fights.

Allstate does not overlook school records, either. In short, Allstate lawyers are instructed to investigate every aspect of a policyholder's life to uncover *any* information that could conceivably embarrass or intimidate them into abandoning the claim or giving in to Allstate's lowball settlement offers. These tactics have proved successful in many cases.

Allstate lawyers are graded, *and rewarded,* on how many cases they take to trial and win.[160] The more aggressively they use these tactics against policyholders, the greater their financial rewards. For Allstate staff lawyers (who are Allstate employees and can only represent Allstate), the financial rewards include bonuses and raises.[161] For retained lawyers (who are hired by Allstate but are not Allstate employees), the financial rewards usually include being hired for more Allstate cases or increases in the hourly fees Allstate is willing to pay them.[162]

Part Two: Motions

The second part of the plan involves the filing of as many motions as possible to overwhelm the plaintiff's attorney with time-consuming, and often unnecessary work. Allstate's plan includes intimidating and discouraging attorneys as well as policyholders from pursuing claims against Allstate. Unfortunately, these tactics have successfully discouraged many attorneys from representing policyholders making claims against Allstate.

Part Three: Pre-Trial Settlement

The third part of the plan involves settlement of the case before trial—or more accurately the *non*-settlement of the case before trial. Allstate lawyers are not allowed to negotiate settlements. The lawyer's job is to follow the adjuster's plan—the low offer we read about in Chapter 9.

The Allstate adjuster controls every aspect of the litigation—not the lawyer. The Allstate adjuster assigns one of four litigation plans to the case before it is assigned to the lawyer.

These litigation plans are:

1. Defend on coverage—zero offer.
2. Defend on liability—zero offer.
3. Defend on damages—zero offer.
4. SFXOL (Settle for X or Litigate)—with the X representing Allstate's computer-generated claim value.[163]

The SFXOL litigation plan is by far the one Allstate assigns most often. The lawyer's job is to tell the policyholder and his or her attorney to settle for Allstate's computer-generated value or else try the case to get any payment from Allstate.

Sample Cases

These facts are taken from published court opinions in actual cases involving Allstate. The similarities in these cases are striking. They are chilling examples of what Allstate's business model will drive insurance companies to do to innocent policyholders in the name of higher profits.

The Tennessee Case

The first case is from Tennessee. In what should have been a simple traffic accident case, the insurer (through their attorneys) asked for an inordinate amount of information. Here is how the Tennessee Supreme Court described the discovery tactics used by Allstate's lawyers in that case:

> As alleged in the plaintiff's complaint, the underlying facts of this case arose out of a 1988 traffic accident involving the plaintiff and the defendant, Larry McElwaney. After the plaintiff filed suit against McElwaney to recover damages, his insurance carrier, Allstate Insurance Company, hired Mr. Hal Nichols, "a highly competent and effective Memphis attorney," to represent McElwaney. Sometime after Mr. Nichols substantially completed discovery in the case, including deposing the plaintiff, submitting interrogatories, and obtaining the plaintiff's medical records, Allstate fired Mr. Nichols and employed the Richardson Law Firm to represent McElwaney.

According to the plaintiff, as soon as Allstate hired the Richardson Firm, the Firm began the discovery process anew to harass her, to cause her to suffer unnecessary expense, and to "weaken [her] resolve to pursue the suit to the extent that she [would] abandon it." The Richardson Firm is first alleged, as an agent of Allstate and McElwaney, to have submitted an excessive number of interrogatories, totaling about 237 questions and subparts, even though it already possessed much of the information requested by the interrogatories.

The plaintiff also alleges that the Richardson Firm deposed her for a second time, subjecting her to "intense questioning about every aspect of her social, educational, employment, and medical history." Lasting about eight hours, this second deposition is alleged to have inquired as to whether the plaintiff "had been sleeping with the Defendant McElwaney," and as to "every ailment with which [she] has ever been beset, no matter how trivial." The plaintiff was also called upon to furnish the names of every doctor, dentist, and other health-care professional who treated her for these ailments.

Further, the Richardson Firm is alleged to have issued more than seventy discovery subpoenas to various records custodians. Despite knowing that many of these records possessed no relevance to the issues in the plaintiff's suit, the Richardson Firm is alleged to have sent subpoenas to:

1. "Every custodian for every healthcare professional who was suspected . . . to have rendered treatment to the plaintiff at any time during her

life," including her psychologist, her obstetrician/gynecologist, and others.

2. Every "hospital in Memphis and Chattanooga (where the plaintiff once lived), even though in many instances[,] the Richardson Firm had no reason to believe that the Plaintiff had received treatment there."

3. Every employer for whom the plaintiff has ever worked.

4. Every automobile repair agency to which the plaintiff's automobile has ever been taken.

5. Every insurance company that has written a policy of insurance for the plaintiff.[164]

Other Cases

Following is a set of anecdotes from other cases that should give you more ideas of the type of "boxing gloves" tactics Allstate regularly uses.

*   In a traffic accident case in New Mexico, Allstate's attorney asked the plaintiff if she had ever been a victim of domestic abuse. This is a potential violation of the Domestic Abuse Insurance Protection Act, and the Insurance Trade Practices and Frauds Act.[165] Allstate also subpoenaed the plaintiff's current employment records, even after they learned that she had been threatened with losing her job because of the hardship the lawsuit caused to her employer.

*   In the same New Mexico traffic accident case, Allstate requested pediatric medical records of an adult plaintiff who was injured. Using this information, they accused the plaintiff of being a drug addict because he had been prescribed Ritalin as a child for Attention Deficit/Hyperactivity Disorder.[166]

117

- In an Indiana case, what should have been a simple unin-sured motorist traffic accident claim turned into more than ten years of litigation with Allstate as they denied the claim and filed motion after motion as a delay tactic.[167]

- In another New Mexico traffic accident case, a policy-holder had good reason to believe that an Allstate claims supervisor used financial information obtained in discov-ery to report a mistake in the policyholder's taxes to the New Mexico tax authorities.[168]

The Results for Policyholders

These cases illustrate McKinsey's "boxing gloves" litigation plan. The object of this plan is intimidation. That means using aggressive tactics to bully both the plaintiff and the plaintiff's attor-ney into walking away or giving up and taking whatever Allstate is offering just to end the agony.

The bottom line for any policyholder or claimant making a legitimate claim against Allstate is this: be prepared to accept about half of what your claim is worth, or endure about four years of investigation and litigation before you see a dime of your money.

It's a strategy that's proved very successful—and profitable. As McKinsey correctly predicted, fewer than 10% of Allstate policy-holders making claims have been willing to enter the kill box of McKinsey's litigation plan. Now that you know what they'd be put through, would you blame them?

12

Colossus

Calibrated to Win the Zero-sum Game

A CENTRAL COMPONENT of McKinsey's "solution" to Allstate's overpayment problem was installing computer evaluation systems. These systems would replace individual adjuster judgments about claim values. Regardless of the unique facts of each claim, the evaluation systems put the same or similar values on all claims of a certain type. I call this McKinsey's one-size-fits-all approach to evaluating claims.

Since auto bodily injury claims are by far the most numerous Allstate handled, McKinsey started its field testing on a computer evaluation system called Colossus in 1994. Colossus was supposed to provide adjusters with uniform values for most auto injury claims—values that also provide the insurer with substantial savings in claim payments.

McKinsey later installed a similar evaluation program called IntegriClaim for CCPR's homeowner's claim protocols. Integri-Claim had the same effect as Colossus—to produce non-negotiable, lowball estimates of property damage. Allstate's IntegriClaim system for Katrina claims, combined with its "Good Hands or Boxing Gloves" negotiation strategy, have been major factors in the slow rate of recovery and the high rate of property abandonment in the Gulf region.[184]

McKinsey's Approach to Evaluating Claims

In our can-of-peas analogy from Chapter 4, we described McKinsey's three-pronged approach to claims as:

1. Automate the factory machinery to under-fill every can of Allstate insurance.

2. Establish new employee performance measurements to reward employees who are able to meet or exceed their sales quotas for Allstate's under-filled cans of insurance.

3. Implement a new high-pressure claims program designed to withhold Allstate's product from customers who need it but are unwilling to accept under-filled cans of insurance for the same high price.

Translated into actual CCPR protocols, McKinsey's three-pronged solution consisted of:

1. Use computer evaluation programs, like Colossus or IntegriClaim, to produce consistent, lowball claim values, regardless of the individual merits of the claim.

2. Enforce employee acceptance of McKinsey's new claim system by establishing performance measurements designed to reward employee behavior that "rewards the shareholders."

3. Enforce policyholder acceptance of reduced claim values by delaying payment to create financial stress. Then give the policyholder a choice between accepting a non-negotiable, lowball offer to get prompt payment—or endure years of expensive litigation to get fair payment.

McKinsey's finding of a supposed 20% overpayment of legitimate claims was another self-fulfilling prophecy. McKinsey already knew that its solution to the evaluation problem for bodily injury claims, the most numerous claims handled by Allstate, would be Colossus. McKinsey chose Colossus because Allstate could calibrate it to instantly reduce all claim values for the most common bodily injury claims by at least 20%—or *any* amount Allstate desired—using the Colossus "tuning process."

What is Colossus?

Colossus is the trade name for a computer program sold and licensed by Computer Sciences Corporation (CSC).[169] Two Australian companies, General Insurance Organization of Australia and Computations Pty Ltd originally developed Colossus between 1988 and 1991.[170] According to Colossus' creators, the intent was to provide consistency in evaluations of the subjective components of injury (also called *general damages*). Traditionally, such evaluations varied based on the experience of the adjuster and the unique facts of the policyholder's injury and circumstances.[171]

The basic premise of Colossus is that by using artificial intelligence programming, the system can calculate a measurement of a person's general damages. Colossus bases this measure on the type of injury, number and type of treatments, and the expected immediate and residual effects of the injury, regardless of the individual characteristics of the person involved.[172]

Colossus produces value ranges for general damages based on a measurement called *severity points*. The program assigns these severity points to all the possible combinations of 600 recognized injury codes, together with the number and types of medical treatments received.[173] Given the same injury details, Colossus assigns the same number of severity points to each claim with very little regard to individual characteristics or non-medical issues such as the real impact of the injury on the policyholder's lifestyle.

The problem with Colossus and its consistency rationale arises from the fundamental nature of casualty coverage. The programmers who created Colossus worked under a state-sponsored system of socialized auto accident reparations, similar to our state workers compensation systems.[174] This is nothing like the American insurance concept of casualty insurance. The insurer who commissioned Colossus did so specifically to cut claim values, which is improper in America, in claims made by a policyholder.

Casualty coverage is supposed to pay *"all* loss resulting from an accident."[175] This is what we discussed in Chapter 3 as the *indemnity principle.* Under the indemnity principle, an insurer bases compensation on the unique extent and nature of the injury for that individual person. The losses suffered by two people in the same accident, even with the same medical diagnosis, will be different. This difference is due to the simple fact that no two people are identical or have identical consequences from the same injury.

By contrast, a *defined benefit coverage* is one that pays a fixed amount for a specified injury regardless of actual losses.[176] This limited benefit feature makes defined benefit policies far less expensive than casualty or indemnity coverages.

How Colossus Works

According to Colossus' creators, they designed the cost calculation mechanism used to create Colossus' severity points around a *central limit theorem,* meaning that claims had an average value based on the injury data.[177] Thus, as its creators explain, Colossus "simply calculates the average risk cost" based on the cases used as examples to set up or "tune" the program.[178]

The implications for applying this calculation mechanism to casualty coverage are significant. For example, if the values of the cases for the calculation range from $0 to $12,000, with an average of $1,299.33, then every claim evaluation based on that database will receive a value of $1,299.33 regardless of the claim's individual characteristics.[179] Claims worth more than $1,299.33 will be undervalued. Claims worth less will be overvalued.

In other words, Colossus does not value any of the claims according to the *actual* losses, which is what casualty coverage is supposed to do under the indemnity principle. When an insurer uses Colossus, they are substituting defined benefit coverage for the casualty coverage the policyholder paid for. To make matters worse, the insurer never informs the policyholders of this critical substitution in coverage. This substitution substantially dilutes the value of the insurance coverage, both when the policyholders buy policies and when they make claims.

When CSC and the insurers who defend their use of Colossus speak of "consistency," what they are really talking about is substituting defined benefit coverage for casualty coverage. They are substituting an average payment for actual restitution. While this idea of consistency has been the argument Allstate uses to justify using Colossus, Colossus' own marketing materials tell the true story.

CSC sales literature touts Colossus as "the most powerful cost savings tool" available to the insurance industry. CSC also tells insurers the program will *immediately* reduce claim payments by up to 20%.[180] The amount of savings Colossus will actually produce is completely flexible according to that insurer's particular needs—meaning that particular insurer's level of greed.

Insurers who license Colossus from CSC pay an initial setup fee of $10 to $30 million with additional monthly maintenance and licensing fees.[181] CSC's marketing materials state that most insurers will completely recover the initial setup costs for Colossus from the savings on claim payments within the first two months.[182] CSC can truthfully make these representations about the amounts and flexibility of the savings Colossus produces because of how Colossus works and how each individual insurer sets it up.

When McKinsey projected to Allstate that Colossus would increase Allstate's casualty profitability by 15% to 20%, McKinsey was betting on a sure thing. McKinsey already knew how Colossus worked, from its experience in the insurance industry.

Colossus Benchmark Tuning

When CSC delivers Colossus to an insurer, the insurer gets a program that calculates severity points for an injury. However, the insurer must first calibrate Colossus through a process called *Benchmark Tuning*. Benchmark tuning is what enables Colossus to "convert severity points into currency."

Using Colossus' benchmark-tuning and fine-tuning programming services, any insurer who buys a license to use Colossus is able to calibrate the amount of savings it wants to generate. McKinsey knew that it would be Allstate, not CSC, who set Colossus' claim values as high or as low as Allstate wanted in comparison with past claim values. This is how McKinsey was able to accurately project that Colossus would immediately increase profits by about 15% to 20%, or as much as $550 to $600 million *per year,* even though this turned out to be a gross underestimation.

The benchmark-tuning process for a region or geographical area begins with the insurer selecting a committee of three to six experienced claim employees. Colossus tuning manuals warn insurers to be very careful about picking the committee for the benchmark-tuning project—they should specifically choose the most experienced and the *most conservative* claim employees available. These employees will become the brains that Colossus will imitate while determining claim values in the region.

This committee then analyzes a group of cases known as benchmark cases. CSC provides these benchmark cases as part of the implementation package. However, CSC provides only eleven cases for the project. Even more incredible, the benchmark-tuning committee then pares these eleven cases down to nine cases for actual input. Thus, Colossus calculates values for every claim in the entire region by referring to a database of just nine claim values.

The benchmark cases are all hypothetical scenarios relating the story of an injury. In each case, the claimant is a 24-year-old white male. The benchmark tuning committee has no information about the claimant's out-of-pocket losses, such as past or future medical bills, past or future wage losses, and so on. The insurer then tells the committee to assume an attorney will not represent the claimant and there is no comparative negligence. *Comparative negligence* is how insurers account for accidents where the claimant is partially at fault. For example, if the claim was worth $10,000 but the claimant was 50% responsible, the claimant would only receive $5,000.

The benchmark committee then considers each of the eleven cases separately and arrives at a consensus figure for each case. This figure represents the most conservative value the group can agree on for general damages. From the eleven values set by the committee, the management selects the most conservative nine cases for input into the Colossus tuning program.

Colossus uses these nine claim values for the algorithm that converts severity points into dollars. In a general sense, this process allows Colossus to determine how many dollars the insurer's employees in this particular region would assign to each severity point. Colossus stores this information and uses it to calculate values for all Colossus-eligible claims in the region.

Colossus Fine Tuning

The results of the benchmark tuning process provide only a starting point for Colossus evaluations. The next step in the Colossus setup process is called *fine tuning*. During this step, the insurer checks Colossus against actual settlements to see if Colossus is generating sufficient savings to meet the insurer's needs. CSC suggests, as a guide, that Colossus should generate at least a 20% savings over the insurer's historical settlement values. This is why CSC can state in its marketing materials that Colossus will generate an immediate 20% savings in claim payments.

The insurer fine-tunes Colossus with what is called a *closed file survey*. The insurer picks closed claim files representing its very best claim settlements. This survey specifically excludes files with attorney representation, policy limits settlements, or jury verdicts. The insurer then runs those eight to sixteen files though the bench-mark-tuned Colossus. After that, the insurer compares the Colossus values to the actual settlement values. If Colossus does not generate sufficient savings to meet the insurer's needs, the insurer simply goes back and adjusts the original benchmark case values downward until Colossus produces the desired results.

Colossus at Allstate

As early as 1993, McKinsey benchmark-tuned Colossus for three Allstate claim offices—Mitchell Field, Woodbury, and North Palm Beach—and found that Colossus was producing values 55% lower than the actual settlements. After they conducted the fine-tuning process and adjusted claim offices in six major economic regions, McKinsey reported "severity reductions" of 10% to 23%.

Based on these and similar benchmark- and fine-tuning tests around the country, McKinsey predictably underestimated that Colossus would produce an "immediate impact" of reducing loss payouts by $225 to $250 million per year. This immediate impact would, of course, come at the immediate expense of Allstate's poli-cyholders.

The Colossus tuning program offered more than just immediate impact. It gave Allstate's regional managers the power to rapidly retune Colossus claim values, and set future profit goals for Allstate's adjusters to meet or beat. Colossus can produce a variety of reports, such as scatter-graphs showing comparisons of actual settlements to Colossus values.

Whenever management perceived any new opportunity to lower claim payouts, they could easily tune Colossus claim evaluations for an entire claim office or region to lower levels. In fact, the McKinsey slides show Allstate employees directly participating in the initial tuning *and* retuning of Colossus for each region in the country.

An Allstate manager can retune a region in less than half an hour without interaction with, or help from, the insurer's computer support staff or CSC employees. Essentially, the regional manager simply enters the desired percentage reduction in claim payments, and Colossus does the rest.

McKinsey created a regional position called Casualty Process Specialist (CPS) to be in charge of retuning Colossus. Allstate has claimed in one New Mexico case that CSC (or perhaps its predecessor Continuum) created a manual entitled the *Advanced CPS Training Manual* specifically to train Allstate CPSs (Casualty Process Specialists) in how to tune a new region, retune a region, or view the results of tuning over time, all without outside help.[183]

Although no literature has yet come into the public about how the IntegriClaim program works, it's safe to assume insurers can manipulate it to produce repair estimates as low as the insurer wants. The Attorney General of Louisiana alleged this in an action filed against a number of the nation's largest insurers, including State Farm, Allstate, and Farmers. The action states that these insurers are skewing home repair estimates with programs like Xactimate and IntegriClaim (which Allstate uses), in order to boost profits. Using these programs, insurers can deliberately underestimate building and rebuilding claims.[184] This must have been one of the reasons McKinsey could predict in 1995 how much its CCPR process would generate in excess profits on homeowner claims during the first three years.

The use of computer evaluation programs to replace individual adjuster judgment and standardize values regardless of the individual merits of the claims, has been a centerpiece of McKinsey's zero-sum game model for the insurance industry. CSC claims that approximately 30 to 40 major insurers are using Colossus.[185]

Centralized computer evaluation systems also mean that adjustors need only limited skills. Hiring adjusters with limited skills allows Allstate to reduce its costs by paying lower salaries to adjusters who handle more claim files. Individual adjuster experience, skill, and judgment don't matter much in McKinsey's CCPR claim environment. The only adjuster skills required under McKinsey's CCPR system are typing data into a computer, and firmly communicating Allstate's non-negotiable settlement offer to the policy-holder.

The impact of computer evaluation programs like Colossus and IntegriClaim on reducing claim payments at Allstate has been dramatic. As stated in previous chapters, Allstate's net operating profits have jumped from an average of $82 million a year to over $2 billion a year since they installed CCPR and Colossus.

13

Allstate on the Gulf Coast

CCPR after Katrina

T HE McKINSEY slides tell the story of how McKinsey designed Allstate's claim factory to produce an inherently defective insurance product. As a result, Allstate sells insurance that is overpriced, and still fails to provide its policyholders with the vital public service they paid for—when they need it most.

Specifically, we can look to tens of thousands of homeowners in Louisiana, Mississippi, and Florida. They put their money and trust in promises of protection which McKinsey's zero-sum game system was designed *not* to deliver. Among the three largest insurers denying Katrina claims, each one has a claim system designed by McKinsey.

McKinsey's business model at Allstate has harmed more than just Allstate's policyholders. Unpaid medical bills are a leading cause of personal bankruptcy across the nation. Unpaid or underpaid homeowners claims affect whole neighborhood, counties, and states when a natural disaster strikes and people who bought insurance can't afford to rebuild. This business model costs American taxpayers billions. Building an insurer's claim system around a zero-sum game creates a corporate culture that encourages dishonest claim practices. Allstate shows this in how it treats both its policy-holders and the American taxpayer in Katrina claims.

Allstate and Flood Insurance

Allstate provided two types of coverage to the homeowners of South Louisiana and New Orleans at the time Katrina hit. The first type was the private homeowner coverage that covered losses caused by wind and hail, such as in a hurricane. However, these policies did not cover damage caused by flood. Under a non-flood homeowner policy, Allstate solely paid the claims for non-flood damages.

At the same time, Allstate also offered its Louisiana policyhold-ers flood insurance through the NFIP, the National Flood Insur-ance Program. The NFIP hires insurers like Allstate to write the flood policies, investigate flood claims, and evaluate flood losses under its Write Your Own (WYO) insurance program. The NFIP then pays for all flood claims which Allstate approves—together with a fee for Allstate based on the gross amount of each flood claim. Those insurer fees range from $60 for an Erroneous Assign-ment claim, up to $5,750 or 2.1% (whichever amount is greater) for each flood claim loss over $250,000.01.

Under this program, the federal government bears all the financial risk. Then, the government pays insurers like Allstate what usually amounts to substantial fees, since floods tend to cause widespread damage to large numbers of homeowners in the affected area. In South Louisiana, Allstate sold both wind policies (where Allstate pays the claims) and flood policies (where the NFIP pays the claims) to thousands of its policyholders.

Consequently, Allstate adjusted a substantial number of Katrina claims where its policyholders had both wind and flood policies. If Allstate's adjuster found that wind caused the damage, then Allstate would have to pay the claim. If Allstate's adjuster found that flood caused the damage, then the NFIP would not only pay the entire claim but would also pay a fee to Allstate based on the gross amount of the flood claim.

Given Allstate's zero-sum game culture, it's not hard to understand what happened in these situations—and why. Evidence uncovered during litigation against Allstate has shown a pattern: Allstate defrauded taxpayers to benefit their shareholders.

For example, there have been numerous instances where Allstate's adjusters may have instructed engineers who inspected a homeowner's property to change their initial reports. If engineers reported that wind caused the damage, they may have changed the reports to find that flood caused the damage. In at least one case, Allstate's engineer determined that flood caused the policyholder's damage before ever actually going to the property.[186]

By changing the engineering reports, Allstate was able to deny claims altogether when the policyholder had no flood coverage. They could also shift the entire loss, or a major portion of the loss, onto the NFIP and the taxpayers. The result: Allstate wins—others must lose. Allstate paid far less on its coverages than it might have if the original engineers' reports had not been changed.[187]

However, Allstate's zero-sum game approach didn't stop there. Because Allstate's fees for flood claims depended on the gross amount of the claim, another pattern typical of Allstate's mentality has begun to surface. As reported in the *New Orleans Times Picayune,* Allstate was apparently charging NFIP *more* for labor and materials on flood claims than it was paying under its own wind coverage for the same labor and materials.

> Allstate seemed to have two different ways of pricing the damage repair costs…If Allstate attributed the damage to wind or rain, for example—putting it (Allstate) on the hook for payment under the customer's homeowner policy—the company priced the cost of removing and replacing the drywall at 76¢ per square foot, *but if the damage was blamed on*

storm surge or flooding, the estimated cost of removing and replacing the drywall more than quadrupled, to $3.31 per square foot. Other similar high charges for water claims and low charges for wind were made for other materials required for the repair.[188]

Inflating labor and material prices for flood claims would also mean higher fees for Allstate from the NFIP. The *Times Picayune* also reported in the same article that, according to adjusters it interviewed for its story, Allstate appeared to be the only insurer doing this in Louisiana for Katrina claims.

In addition, evidence introduced during trial in *Weiss v. Allstate*,[189] suggests that Allstate's adjusters may have been changing contents loss reports on claims labeled as *flood* to increase Allstate's fees. The evidence suggests Allstate adjusters altered the contents loss forms which the policyholders submitted, without the policyholders' knowledge, to reflect more losses. This would increase the gross amount of the claim and therefore increase Allstate's fees. Such conduct is directly traceable to the zero-sum game culture at Allstate. Even more shocking, the company who operates the NFIP for the federal government is CSC, the same company that licenses Colossus to Allstate, and which has Allstate executives on its advisory council.

We may never know how many billions of dollars in extra prof its Allstate gained for its shareholders and executives during the Katrina disaster by underpaying its own claims or by dumping its liability onto the taxpayer-funded NFIP. Under the Bush administration, the Department of Justice has shown no apparent interest in investigating or criminally prosecuting any of these allegations. Given the department's recently documented partisan partiality, their lack of interest may be due in some part to the fact that the insurance industry has been a major supporter and contributor to the Republican business agenda over the past ten years.

However, insurance denials hurt everyone, regardless of political affiliation. Former Republican Senator Trent Lott of Mississippi lost a home due to Katrina, and has become an outspoken critic of Allstate and State Farm.[190] We can only hope that such criticism will grow as the public becomes aware of these problems.

14

Redefining the Game

Putting Policyholders Back Where They Belong

W HAT CAN we do about this kind of conduct by one of our largest insurers? This behavior erodes the financial safety net that Allstate and other insurers were licensed to provide to policyholders.

Attorneys for Consumer Protection

Attorneys who represent policyholders serve as the final guard to protect the public from the kind of conduct this book describes. My colleagues who fight these battles do it as a personal calling, not for fame or money (although that's what Allstate and McKinsey would like you to believe). Consumer attorneys who work in insurance law spend years dedicated to bad-faith cases, reading and processing hundreds of thousands of documents. Not only do they advocate for the people they represent, but in uncovering inappropriate insurer conduct, they protect members of the public who someday may make a claim.

However, no good deed goes unpunished. Consumer attorneys face hostility from the same public they try to protect. Conditioned by the media, as McKinsey designed in the "Winning the Economic Game" slide shown on page 87, jurors often reject claims their neighbors make for legitimate injuries. When you read that slide on page 87, and realize the extent to which McKinsey and All-state orchestrated public attitudes toward attorneys, you can begin to see you've been pawns in McKinsey's game. You might be playing along in McKinsey's game when you serve on a jury and turn someone away, when you believe people who have to sue are greedy, when you defame attorneys who protect injured people, or when you support the agendas of organizations whose purpose is to malign attorneys. The result is all the same; you have believed a lie.

Some day, your claim may be denied, or you may be treated with an insurer's boxing gloves. If that happens you will likely do the same thing as former Republican Senator Trent Lott did when his house was destroyed in Hurricane Katrina, and State Farm denied his property claim. You'll hire an attorney.

All the while, insurers have lobbied courts and legislatures to ensure that jurors never know insurance is at stake in injury cases. Insurers have an incentive to make low offers and then stay out of sight while their policyholders get sued. Remember the *third-party claimant* described in Chapter 9? If you accidentally injure someone else, that injured person is the *third party*, covered under *your* insurance. If that third party gets a low offer and goes to court, to the jury, the third party is suing *you*, not your insurer. Behind the scenes, however, the insurer hires the attorney and uses the tactics described in this book. This creates an artificial surge in litigation; not from frivolous lawsuits, but instead, from frivolous denials of legitimate claims.

Insurers have also lobbied to make sure juries don't hear about insurer settlement tactics. The jury is left with an impression that despite the defendant's best efforts to resolve a case by offering plenty of money, the injured party was so greedy, he sued the poor person who hurt him. As you've read, the reality is quite different. Much of the time, an injured person has to sue because the insurance company is giving him the "boxing gloves" treatment and offering little or nothing. If the injured person is seriously hurt, and his treatment lasts beyond the "Good Hands" threshold, he automatically gets treated with boxing gloves.

The last few years have been particularly lucrative for the insurance industry. McKinsey, through its tactics at Allstate, and through its connections with much of the Fortune 500, has made the term *trial lawyer* evoke the idea of an enemy of society. They have effectively turned the American public against a source of real protection from insurance companies. McKinsey and its followers have turned the American right to access the courts into an issue of "tort reform," evoking the thought that anyone who sues is an "abuser" of the system. They have framed a vision of the judicial system being wildly out of control. Through the media, McKinsey's clients have convinced us the legal system must be "reformed." While they have conditioned us to believe that frivolous lawsuits are clogging the courthouses, the number of civil litigation cases for personal injury are down substantially from their levels in 1992 in both state and federal courts. Moreover, jury verdicts in auto injury cases are at levels below where they were in the 1980s, despite medical costs associated with those cases that have increased by 6% *per year* since then.[191]

The call for tort reform, combined with Allstate's litigation tactics, have accomplished McKinsey's plan. Economics have driven many attorneys out of the courtroom because they can't afford to try cases for smaller injuries. Allstate drags cases on as long as possible to drive up costs. Allstate wins if both the injured person and his or her attorney lose money when they try to file an injury claim. If an attorney can sustain the financial pressure of dragging cases out for years, Allstate then relies on tort-reformed jurors to turn away the injured person with nothing. In these ways, lower offers and suspicious juries lead to lower verdicts and less incentive to try cases. The word spreads. Access to justice narrows.

That's where you come in. Insurers rely on social conditioning; they expect you to view your neighbors as greedy because they request compensation for injuries. What jurors have been conditioned to disregard is that $0 for a legitimate injury equals zero justice. Half of fair compensation equals a half-justice. Only in compensating another member of your community at the full value of the worth for their loss, is any justice provided.

Insurers put an injured person's life under a microscope. They call courtroom doctors (who work for insurers most of the time), former friends, or former flames, to slander the injured person's character. They go to great lengths to ensure that the experience in the litigation "kill box" with Allstate is memorable. So memorable, that injured people tell their friends and neighbors, and the attorney tells his or her colleagues, that litigation with Allstate simply isn't worth it. The scorched earth defense has worked beautifully.

In the process, what have these tactics done? For one, they have driven people into bankruptcy as a result of unpaid medical bills. That puts a larger burden on you, the taxpayer. People are left disabled, but without compensation to support them. They require social services—funded by you. This process is called privatizing profit and socializing loss.

For those few attorneys facing years of litigation in a bad-faith case like the one Allstate created for the Pincheiras, the payouts (if there are any) generally break down to about minimum wage once the attorney calculates all lawyer and staff hours. There are exceptions, of course, but not many. I have calculated that I have received around $5.30 per hour for the time I have put into informing the public about this issue. That's certainly nothing compared to the $27,400,000,000 I calculate Allstate's pre-tax income has increased under CCPR.

Recent cases by a conservative U.S. Supreme Court have taken away effective economic penalties for insurers engaged in improper or even outrageous conduct. Punitive damages (amounts requested by lawyers to deter bad conduct) have been limited by the U.S.

138

Supreme Court in cases such as *State Farm v. Campbell* [192] and *Williams v. Philip Morris.*[193] These cases send a clear message that no matter how bad an insurer's conduct might be, a jury verdict can't be high enough to create a deterrence to the insurer's behavior.

The public is only vaguely aware that many of the largest verdicts they read about in the news are appealed, and end up being resolved years later for pennies on the dollar. Because U.S. Supreme Court justices are appointed for life, and the recent decisions on punitive damages serve as legal precedent for all future cases, this impact may be felt for the next hundred years or more. The only real way to effect change is through legislation, grass roots efforts, your voting choices, and your service as jurors.

Those who push "tort reform" would have you believe that any injured person seeking compensation is greedy, lazy, or doesn't want to work any more. That they are looking for "jackpot justice" or a "free ride" in life. Instead, our judicial system has evolved so that we compensate with money, because money is what our country has chosen to use. The oldest code of law, the Code of Hammurabi, discussed in religious texts such as the Torah, the Old Testament of the Bible, and the Koran, supports a system of justice that uses "an eye for an eye" for compensation. Some countries continue this today. However, we're a civilized society that has evolved past this method of justice. We've chosen money to compensate people for their injuries when someone else is at fault. We recognize that money is an imperfect solution to a complex problem. But it's all we have. The only purpose for insurance is that we have chosen a monetary compensation system. Insurance replaces the monetary value of the injured person's loss. If you think money is a bad way to compensate people, consider the alternative. However, that system will only work so long as insurers and jurors actually compensate people fully.

What Can We Do?

First, and probably most important, states need to address insurance reform legislation. This country needs stronger state legislation to make insurers financially accountable: to policyholders, and to the public they are licensed to serve. We need law that *requires* insurers to lower premiums when, as in Allstate's case, record profits are flooding in at the same time the company is consistently paying out substantially less for claims than industry peers.

States also need to enact laws that prevent insurers from using improper claims practices. This is called a *private right of action in tort* for violations of the Uniform Claims Practices Act, for both first- and third-party claims. At present, several states do not allow policyholders to sue their own insurance companies for intentional underpayment, improper delay, or improper denials. In other words, in these states, your insurance company can do absolutely anything they want to you, and you have no right to take legal action.

On a national level, Congress could address the insurance industry's partial exemption from price-fixing and anti-trust laws. If personal auto insurance and homeowners' insurance markets were truly competitive, as insurers claim, why should a major national insurer be able to charge excessive rates and reap enormous profits over an extended period? How could an insurer making record profits ask for or justify price increases when its competitors are lowering their prices? The fact may be that insurers are no longer competing. They are turning our claims into secret revenue streams to keep ever-larger share of our monthly premiums.

In a truly competitive market, insurers would compete, at least in part, on price. A company that charged excessive prices and realized unreasonable profits as a result should find itself losing business to companies willing to charge less. This hasn't been the case with Allstate. Competition between the major insurers is proving to be a myth. Most major insurers have set very similar payouts on claims using Colossus and other claims software systems, so their competitive edge has to come from an increase in non-accommodating claim-handling tactics.

What can policyholders do? First, policyholders could vote with their feet by deserting Allstate and companies using similar tactics. Switching to another insurance company is one answer. But which one? Consumers can use several ways to check how an insurer is treating its policyholders. However, all require the consumer to make an effort. Fortunately, non-industry sources of information are available, some on the internet, for consumers to get honest information about insurers' quality.

The Consumer Federation of America and the article by J. Robert Hunter cited in this book are certainly valuable sources for accurate information (http://www.consumerfed.org). Another excellent resource is United Policyholders (http://www.unitedpoli cyholders.org).

United Policyholders is doing a tremendous job for insurance consumers across the country. Among United Policyholders' activities, it provides useful advice on how to buy insurance or make a claim; it lobbies for legislation to protect policyholders; and it files *amicus curia* (friend of the court) briefs in courts around the country on issues important to policyholders. These lengthy amicus briefs are filed on behalf of all policyholders. These attorneys almost always do this *pro bono publico* (for the good of the public) without any pay.

One United Policyholders publication for people who face a catastrophic loss of their home, *The Disaster Recovery Handbook & Household Inventory Guide* (U.P. Press 2006), is especially relevant for homeowners today. In this book, authors Amy Bach and Carol Ingalls Custodio have created an invaluable aid for anyone going through the life-altering trauma of losing a home, whether or not the loss is part of a greater natural disaster. The authors give solid, practical advice to the policyholder, including numerous valuable resources for finding independent help when help is needed the most.

As an experienced insurance attorney, I recommend this book to policyholders who are already dealing with the loss of their home. I also recommend it to attorneys who want to handle such claims, and to policyholders who want to be prepared in case the unthinkable should happen to them. Natural disasters are becoming more frequent and the insurance industry is shifting toward McKinsey's business model. The information in this book couldn't come at a more opportune time for both policyholders and the attorneys who represent them.

In addition, consumers can inquire about consumer complaints at their state insurance regulator's office. Consumer complaints are usually considered public records. A consumer can contact the local state insurance regulator's office and ask about the number of complaints that consumers make against particular companies. Keep in mind that many people consider such complaints impractical, because state insurance departments lack the resources, political will, and authority to be the decider in individual claim disputes.

According to The Consumer Federation of America, when compared to other insurers with annual premiums over $1 billion, Allstate ranked second nationwide in both 2005 and 2006 in consumer complaints about its handling of auto claims. Liberty Mutual had the most complaints.[194] For homeowner claims, Allstate came in second nationwide in 2005 and first in 2006 for the number of complaints against insurers with annual premiums over $1 billion. Farmers came first in 2005.[195]

Another action consumers can take is to shop by premium price. However, the consumer must be cautious here. A lower price doesn't necessarily mean the same level of protection. A lower premium might be due to the policy providing less coverage than another company's policy offers. In other words, losses covered by one insurer's policy might be excluded from coverage under a cheaper policy.

In the end, however, the most powerful defense against insurance schemes like McKinsey's zero-sum game is public information. As is often said, sunlight is the best disinfectant for dishonest practices. Public awareness may be the force that brings an end to McKinsey's methods in the insurance industry.

Now that Allstate has disclosed the McKinsey slides, the public can know know about the dangers of Allstate's insurance product. Like any product, companies that sell insurance should be required to disclose their product's contents, behavior, and what the public can expect from it, or else be forced to withdraw it from the market. That, ultimately, is the point of this book.

Epilogue

F OR TEN years, Allstate steadfastly refused to allow any public access to the documents on which this book is based—the McKinsey documents. On April 4, 2008, just as this book was about to be published, the senior executives at Allstate's headquarters in Northbrook, Illinois, made an extraordinary decision. They published 150,000 McKinsey documents on their corporate website.

During the years Allstate tried to restrict access to the documents, Allstate's current Assistant Vice President of Claims, Christine Sullivan, filed dozens of affidavits in state and federal courts around the country. In all these nearly identical affidavits, Sullivan swore under oath that these documents contained highly valuable, confidential, commercial information. This information describes how Allstate developed and operates the CCPR claim handling system.

Sullivan also swore that the information in these documents was so critical and so valuable to Allstate that public release of this information would severely damage Allstate's business. In fact, Sullivan continued to file these affidavits throughout 2007.

Using these affidavits, Allstate convinced judges and appellate courts to prohibit public access to these documents. The first judge I'm aware of to reject Sullivan's claims and allow public access to these documents was Judge Art Encinias in Santa Fe, New Mexico. That series of events is outlined in Chapter 1.

As this book describes, Allstate never obeyed Judge Encinias' order, and was held in contempt of court for its refusal. Seven years later, as I wrote this book, that order was still on appeal in the New Mexico Supreme Court.

Allstate has also refused to obey similar orders from courts in other states. On October 6, 2006, in an Indiana case, Allstate's refusal to obey resulted in a jury verdict against it for $20 million.[196] On August 28, 2007, a Missouri judge sanctioned Allstate for its similar refusal with a $25,000 per day fine.[197] That fine continued to grow with each passing day. It now exceeds $4 million.

On January 16, 2008, the Florida Office of Insurance Regulation suspended Allstate's license to write new insurance policies in Florida because Allstate again refused to publicly produce the McKinsey documents, among others, in response to a subpoena from the department.[198]

On January 19, 2008, an Allstate stockholder filed a federal lawsuit against Allstate and its top executives, including new CEO Thomas Wilson and recently retired Chairman Edward Liddy.[199] The suit alleges that Allstate's executives are hurting Allstate's business and the value of its stock by refusing to publicly produce the McKinsey documents. Allstate's refusal to produce the documents is in contempt of court orders and in defiance of the Florida insurance department's subpoena. The result of this refusal is substantial fines, penalties, and the suspension of its license to do business in Florida. The suit also alleges that the Florida market alone generated nearly $2 billion in revenues for Allstate in 2006.[200]

On January 18, 2008, Allstate appealed the suspension of its Florida license and won a temporary stay of its suspension. On

April 4, 2008, the Florida court of appeals issued its opinion. This opinion affirms the suspension of Allstate's license to do business in Florida, effective immediately.

That same day, Allstate's top executives made one of the most spectacular about-faces in insurance industry history. On April 4, 2008, at approximately 6:00 p.m., central time, Allstate issued a "media release" announcing it was posting approximately 150,000 McKinsey documents on its corporate website. The public now has full access to these documents. As a result, you can now see them for yourself at http://media.allstate.com/categories/52/releases/4390.

As a result of this startling turnaround, the years of legal battles over public disclosure of the McKinsey documents are probably over. The events described in this book have forced the country's second largest insurance company to make an unprecedented concession to the public's right know how their claims are being handled.

Glossary

casualty insurance. Insurance that most consumers buy for their possessions. Includes homeowners insurance, auto insurance, and renter's insurance. Casualty insurance does not include such insurance types as medical, life, or long-term care.

casualty insurance industry average. The average amounts from each premium dollar that support various parts of the casualty insurance business. Typically, 25¢ is for the insurance company's overhead and expenses, 70¢ is for paying claims, and 5¢ is for profit.

CCPR (Claims Core Process Redesign). A redesign of the claims processes at Allstate which McKinsey and Company designed.

combined net income. The combination of that year's net *operating income* (what's left over at the end of the year from earned premiums, after paying all the claims and expenses), plus the investment income from investing earned premiums, reserves, and the insurer's *surplus.*

duty of good faith. The duty every insurer owes by law to its customers to treat them honestly at all times, and to pay their legitimate claims promptly and fairly. The duty of good faith requires the insurer to give its customers' interests the same consideration it gives to its own interests.

expenses and overhead. The portion of the insurer's premium dollar reserved for operating expenses. Typically, this is 25¢ of the premium dollar. Operating expenses include staff salaries, office expenses, computers, marketing, and so on.

fiduciary principle. The standard governing how an insurer should behave while exercising its control over the fund of premium money it collects to pay legitimate claims. By accepting its customers' premiums, the insurer agrees to hold this fund of money in trust for the benefit of its customers, and to pay all legitimate claims from that fund. Because this fund belongs to the customers, and not the insurer, the insurer has a duty to pay all legitimate claims promptly, and not to withhold payment unreasonably.

first-party claims. A claim for expenses when a policyholder experiences a loss. The policyholder is the *first party*, the person who purchased the policy and pays the premiums. A person who makes a first-party claim is also called a *first-party claimant*.

indemnity/fiduciary principle. A combination of the insurer's duties to pay claims fairly (to *indemnify* the insured, or make them whole again), and promptly (to fulfill their *fiduciary* duty when they hold their customers' money in trust).

indemnity insurance. The type of insurance which promises to *indemnify*, or make whole again. If the insured experiences a covered loss, indemnity insurance pays all covered expenses rather than a flat fee. These expenses can vary from person to person, depending on their individual injuries, damages, and circumstances.

indemnity principle. The insurer's duty to pay the full costs of an insured's loss and put them back in the same financial position they were before the loss.

investment income. Income the insurer earns from investing the accumulated money held in trust for claims, plus the company's surplus.

insured. See *policyholder.*

joint claims account. A concept that illustrates how policyholders' money is held in trust. Like a joint bank account, the joint claims account represents the combined money of all policyholders.

loss costs. The portion of the insurance premium that an insurer expects to pay out for covered losses during the course of the policy year. For most casualty insurers, this averages to about 70¢ of the premium dollar.

loss ratio. An insurance company's *loss ratio* is the incurred losses divided by premiums collected. Calculating the loss ratio is one way to determine the value of insurance coverage—the loss ratio shows what portion of an insurer's premiums returns to the policyholders in covered claims.

loss reserves. See *reserves.*

MCO. Allstate's abbreviation for Market Claims Office. The McKinsey slides refer to several market claims offices at various locations during the implementation and testing of CCPR.

net operating income. For an insurer, this is the money left over after collecting the premiums, paying the claims, and paying the company's expenses.

policyholder. The insurer's customer—the person who purchased the insurance policy and pays the monthly premiums.

premium. The monthly or yearly fee that a policyholder pays for insurance coverage.

premium profit. The portion of the premium dollar that the insurer sets aside for profit. Typically 5¢ of the premium dollar.

pure loss ratio. See *loss ratio.*

quasi-public nature of insurance. Like a utility, an insurance company is a business that operates under license to serve the public. An ordinary business such as a retailer can fluctuate with the market, operate how they please, and even go out of business. An insurance company, by contrast, holds the public's money in trust, and must remain solvent and serve the public in the way for which it is licensed.

reserves. The amount of money set aside in reserve for claims incurred or known to be due but not yet paid.

shareholders. Investors who have purchased stock in a publicly traded company. Their interest is in the financial health of the company, in order to gain a return on their investment.

surplus. The accumulation of all the insurer's past profits and investments.

third-party claims. Insurance claims for damaged property or injuries that the policyholder caused. Examples include an injured person in an auto accident when the insured is at fault, or a damaged car when the insured is at fault. People who make claims against policies they did not purchase are called *third-party claimants*.

traditional rules of casualty insurance. A collection of rules, laws, and codes of conduct built up over the past hundred years that govern how insurers treat their customers when there is a covered loss.

trustee. A person or entity that holds money or property for the benefit of others. The trustee holds the assets and is often paid a fee for their services, but does not have the right to benefit personally from the assets.

People

Robert Block. Allstate's Vice President of Investor Relations in 2006.

Jerry Choate. In 1992, at the beginning of the CCPR project, Jerry Choate was the Senior Executive Vice President of Claims at Allstate. In 1994, Choate became Allstate's President and CEO. In 1995, Choate was promoted to Allstate's Chairman of the Board, where he served until his retirement in 1999. The McKinsey slides suggest that Choate was instrumental in hiring McKinsey, and he was present in many of the early presentations.

Judge Art Encinias. Judge in the case *Pincheira v. Allstate Ins. Co.* which led to uncovering the McKinsey slides.

Dan Hale. Allstate's Chief Financial Officer (CFO) in 2006 and 2007.

J. Robert Hunter. Mr. Hunter is a consulting actuary with over 40 years of experience with the insurance industry. He is a Fellow of the Casualty Actuarial Society and a member of the American Academy of Actuaries. From 1970 to 1980, Mr. Hunter served as Chief Actuary and Federal Insurance Administrator for the Federal Insurance Administration. From 1993 to 1994, Mr. Hunter served as the Insurance Commissioner for the State of Texas. Since 1994, Mr. Hunter has served as the Director of Insurance for the Consumer Federation of America, a federation of some 240 consumer advocacy groups with a combined membership of more than 50 million Americans. Mr. Hunter has also published dozens of major articles and reports on the insurance industry and testified numerous times as an expert on insurance industry practices and premiums before committees of both the U.S. Congress and the U.S. Senate as well as the legislatures of every State.

Edward Liddy. Senior Vice President and Chief Financial Officer (CFO) of Sears until 1993. Allstate's President and CEO from 1995 to 1999. Became Allstate's Chairman of the Board in 1999, replacing Jerry Choate. Retired in 2007.

José Pincheira. An Allstate policyholder who was injured (along with his wife, Olivia) in an auto accident. Allstate denied proper coverage, and as a result Mr. Pincheira hired this book's author, David J. Berardinelli to represent him in a case against Allstate. That case uncovered the McKinsey slides.

Olivia Pincheira. An Allstate policyholder, wife of José Pincheira.

Ethan Rasiel. Author of *The McKinsey Way*, a book based on his experiences as a McKinsey consultant from 1989 to 1992.

Jeffrey Skilling. Former McKinsey partner who became CEO of Enron in 1996. Stepped down as Chairman and CEO on August 18, 2001. Was convicted on May 26, 2006 of multiple counts of conspiracy, fraud, false statements, and insider trading. Is currently serving a 24-year sentence in federal prison in Minnesota.

Judge Michael Vigil. Replaced Judge Art Encinias part way through the *Pincheira* case when Judge Encinias retired.

Thomas Wilson. Allstate's CEO in 2007.

Notes

Introduction

1   J. Robert Hunter, *Congressional Testimony of J. Robert Hunter,* June 21, 2001, Subcommittee on Capital Markets, Insurance and Government Sponsored Enterprises of the Financial Services Committee: http://financialservices.house.gov/media/pdf/062101hu.pdf.

See "J. Robert Hunter" on page 153.

2   J. Robert Hunter, "The "Good Hands" Company Or A Leader In Anti-Consumer Practices?—Excessive Prices and Poor Claims Practices at The Allstate Corporation," *Consumer Federation of America Report* (July 18, 2007), 15 (footnotes omitted). Hereafter referenced as "Hunter."

3   I graduated from Santa Clara University Law School in 1974 and was admitted to practice law in New Mexico on October 9, 1974. For the first five years of my career, I worked as an Assistant District Attorney prosecuting criminal cases in Santa Fe, New Mexico, the town I was born in. After leaving the District Attorney's office in 1980, I started my own law practice in Santa Fe and have practiced on my own ever since.

4   David J. Berardinelli, "False Promises—Allstate, McKinsey and the Zero Sum Game," *The New Mexico Trial Lawyer* 93 (Aug. 2005), 35-4. The "False Promises" article has been reprinted with permission in legal journals in Arizona, California, Colorado, Illinois, Kentucky, Montana, Ohio, Texas, Washington, and West Virginia.

David J. Berardinelli, "An Insurer In The Grip Of Greed," *Trial Magazine*, American Association for Justice (July 2007), 43-7.

David J. Berardinelli, et al., *From Good Hands to Boxing Gloves: How Allstate Changed Casualty Insurance in America* (legal edition, Trial Guides 2006, 2008).

5   Michael Orey, "In Tough Hands at Allstate," *BusinessWeek* (May 1, 2006), http://www.businessweek.com/@@bYW8@mcQUSQ2Oh4A/premium/content/06_18/b3982072.htm/

Brandon Ortiz, "Allstate Accused Of Cheating Claimants," *Lexington Herald-Leader,* July 10, 2006, http://www.kentucky.com/mld/kentucky/news/14998199.htm

Drew Griffin, Kathleen Johnston, "Auto Insurers Play Hardball In Minor-Crash Claims," *CNN,* February 9, 2007 http://www.cnn.com/2007/US/02/09/insurance.hardball/index.html

Walter Updegrave, Kate Ashford, "Think You're Insured? Maybe Not," *Money Magazine,* May 1, 2007 http://money.cnn.com/magazines/moneymag/moneymag_archive/2007/03/01/8400877/index.htm

David Dietz, Darrell Preston, "Home Insurers' Secret Tactics Cheat Fire Victims, Hike Profits," *Bloomberg Magazine,* August 3, 2007, http://www.bloomberg.com/apps/news?pid=20601170&refer=home&sid=aIOpZROwhvNI

Bloomberg News, Interview on the McKinsey Documents, August 14, 2007 http://www.bloomberg.com/apps/ news?pid=20601170&refer=home&sid=aIOpZROwhvNI

David Brancaccio, Brenda Breslauer, "Home Insurance 9-1-1," *NOW on the News,* PBS, August 17, 2007, http:// www.pbs.org/now/shows/333/insurance-industry.html

Rebecca Mowbray, "Allstate's Dirty Secrets Revealed, Lawyer Claims," *The New Orleans Times-Picayune,* August 22, 2007, http://www.nola.com/timespic/stories/index.ssf?/base/ money-1/118776405969200.xml&coll=1

Chapter 1: The Story Behind the Story

6   *Pincheira, et al., v. Allstate Ins. Co., et al.,* D-0101-CV-2000-2894.

7   *Pincheira, et al. vs. Allstate Ins. Co., et al.,* D-0101-CV-99-00145, Deposition of Sylvia Encinias, 65-69, 82-88, October 18, 1999. If this is what Allstate was training its agents to tell policyholders, as Ms. Encinias repeatedly said, then it was apparently in a CCPR related effort to save money. This induced ignorant policyholders to reject the broader coverage (UM coverage), under which Allstate would have to pay higher amounts in claims, and accept a less valuable coverage (medical payments) under which Allstate's claim payments would be significantly reduced.

8   Deposition of Toni M. Boyd, Senior Manager (Home Office), who was a leader and team member of the Homeowner CCPR redesign team, and who states she was involved in the CCPR homeowner design process from July 1996 to January 2000. *Gilmore v. Allstate Insurance Company, et al.,* No. 2000-32830 CICI, Seventh Judicial District, Volusia County, Florida, October 17, 2002, at p 16-33.

9   David J. Berardinelli, "False Promises—Allstate, McKinsey, and the Zero Sum Game," *The New Mexico Trial Lawyer,* 93.

10 *Martinez et al. v. Allstate Ins. Co., et al.,* D-0101-CV-2004-0963; *Fields v. Allstate Insurance Company,* 45C01-9501-CT-01927.

11 Florida Office of Insurance Regulation, "Florida Insurance Commissioner Suspends Allstate Insurance Co.," http://www.floir.com/pressreleases/viewmediarelease.aspx?id=2858 (accessed January 17, 2008). The Florida Commissioner is investigating whether Allstate's current request for a massive increase in its Florida car insurance premiums is justified in light of Allstate's record breaking profits over the past ten years. Allstate no longer sells homeowner insurance in Florida. Allstate's string of record-breaking annual profits will be discussed in more detail later in this book.

12 Ibid.

Chapter 2: The McKinsey Business Credo

13 Wikipedia, "Gordon Gekko," http://en.wikipedia.org/wiki/Gordon_Gekko. "While the producers of the movie Wall Street clearly intended to portray this character as a villain; ironically enough, thanks to this movie, Gordon Gekko became a source of inspiration for a countless number of investment bankers around the world. It has often been suggested that Wall Street turned out to be a most effective recruitment tool for the investment banking industry."

14 John Byrne, "Inside McKinsey," *BusinessWeek,* July 8, 2002, http://www.businessweek.com/magazine/content/02_27/b3790001.htm. Hereafter referenced as "Byrne."

15 Ibid.

16 Ibid.

17 Ibid.

18 Allstate, "2007 Notice of Annual Meeting/Proxy Statement/2006 Annual Report," Allstate reports its stock value rose by 115.66% through 2006, whereas the stock value of all prop-

erty-casualty insurers rose by 60.58%. During the same period, the Standard & Poor's 500 index increased by 35.43%.

19 Robert Ringer, "The Desire to Acquire," *World Net Daily Commentary* (February 1, 2007), http://www.wnd.com/news/article.asp?ARTICLE_ID=54033.

20 See the McKinsey slide reproduced on page 83.

21 Trial Testimony of Alan J. Hapke, Property Casualty Actuary, Fellow of the American Academy of Actuaries, Fellow of the Casualty Actuary Society, 26-28, June 29, 1995, *King et al. v. Providence Washington Ins. Co.,* et al., SF 91-141(C).

Deposition of Alan Sealy, Head Actuary New Mexico Department of Insurance, *Armijo v. Allstate Indem. Co.,* D-0101-CV-2002-0318, February 28, 2005, 43-44, agreeing that loss costs are "in the ballpark" of 70% of auto insurance premiums.

Deposition of Richard Biondi, Head Commercial Auto Actuary for Insurance Services Office (ISO), *King et al. v. Providence Washington Ins. Co., et al.,* SF 91-141(C), April 11, 1995, 184-85, 194-95. Mr. Biondi stated that casualty insurance premiums consist of three charges: loss costs, operating or overhead expenses, and profit. About 30% of all casualty premiums represent the insurer's charges for both expenses and profit— meaning loss costs represent about 70% of casualty premiums.

22 *Weiss v. Allstate Insurance Company,* 06-CV-3774, Joint Trial Exhibit 7, Memo re Media Requests & Key Messages, August 31, 2005, at ALST-WEIS 0972.

Chapter 3: Traditional Insurance Rules

23 Harvey W. Rubin, *Dictionary of Insurance Terms,* (3rd ed. Barron's 1995), 218. "Indemnity [is] compensation for loss. In a property and casualty contract, the objective is to restore an insured to the same financial position after the loss that he or she was in prior to the loss. But the insured should not be able to

profit by damage or destruction of property, nor should the insured be in a worse financial position after a loss."

24 *German Alliance Ins. Co. v. Lewis,* 233 U.S. 389, 414-15 (1914) (emphasis added); State ex rel. *St. Louis Mut. Life Ins. Co. v. Mulloy,* 330 Mo. 951, 52 S.W.2d 469 (Mo., Jun 15, 1932). "The insurance business, like that of banking, is peculiarly dependent upon public trust and confidence."

25 *Webster's New Collegiate Dictionary* (1981), 1246. "… a natural or legal person to whom property is legally committed to be administered for the benefit of a beneficiary."

26 Harvey W. Rubin, *Dictionary Of Insurance Terms* (Barron's 3rd ed. 1995), 242.

Chapter 4: Insurance and the Can of Mother's Peas

27 *Zilisch v. State Farm Mutual Auto. Ins. Co.,* 995 P.2d 276, 280 (Ariz. 2000) "The carrier has an obligation to immediately conduct an adequate investigation, act reasonably in evaluating the claim, and act promptly in paying a legitimate claim. It should do nothing that jeopardizes the insured's security under the policy. *It should not force an insured to go through needless adversarial hoops to achieve its rights under the policy.* It cannot lowball claims or delay claims hoping that the insured will settle for less. Equal consideration of the insured requires more than that." (emphasis added).

28 Hunter (Note 2, *supra*), 1-2.

29 Ibid., 13.

30 Ibid., 11.

31 "Allstate's Earnings Fall Short As Profits Rise," *New York Times,* July 17, 2007. http://www.nytimes.com/2007/07/19/business/19allstate.html?ex=1189051200&en=32145a4783b0ece2&ei=5070. "Allstate said operating earnings, *which analysts*

use to measure performance because they exclude investments, were $1.07 billion, or $1.76 a share." (emphasis added).

32 *Best's Key Rating Guide,* (1991 Ed.), 20; *Best's Key Rating Guide,* (1995 Ed.), 24. Again, these figures are rounded off. The precise figures for the years 1986 through 1994 from *Best's* are: $2,247,926,000 in total net income for an average yearly net income (over nine years) of $224,792,600.

33 *Best's Key Rating Guide* for 1999, 2003, 2005; *Best's Key Rating Guide,* (1999 Ed.), 22; *Best's Key Rating Guide,* (2003 Ed.), 26; *Best's Key Rating Guide,* (2005 Ed.), 30.

34 "4 Investigates: Has Allstate reduced claims in an effort to increase profits? Part 1," WWL-TV, New Orleans, Louisiana, November 6, 2007, http://www.wwltv.com/local/stories/wwl110607jbinsurance.1e62c5e0e.html

"4 Investigates: Did Allstate betray policyholders by cutting claims to boost profits? Part 2," WWL-TV, New Orleans, Louisiana, November 7, 2007, http://www.wwltv.com/local/stories/wwl110607jbinsurance.1e62c5e0e.html.

35 "4 Investigates: Did Allstate betray policyholders by cutting claims to boost profits? Part 2," WWL-TV, New Orleans, Louisiana, November 7, 2007, http://www.wwltv.com/local/stories/wwl110607jbinsurance.1e62c5e0e.html. According to Mr. Halberg, Allstate increased its total car and homeowner policies from 20.8 million in 1996 to a total of 25.9 million in 2006.

36 Ibid.

37 Allstate Corporation Notice of Annual Meeting and Proxy Statement (3/28/03) – D1-D2; Allstate Corporation Notice of Annual Meeting and Proxy Statement (3/26/01) – D2-D3; Allstate Corporation Notice of Annual Meeting and Proxy Statement (3/27/00), A2-A3; Allstate Corporation 1994 Annual Report, 33; Allstate Corporation 1997 Summary Annual Report, 22-23.

Best's Review (October 1996), 34; *Best's Review* (December 1995), 20.

38   Hunter (Note 2, *supra*), 1-2.

39   Ibid., 1.

40   "Allstate's profits were consistently higher than that of the overall industry during this period [1987-2006], averaging about 6% more." Ibid., 2.

41   Allstate Corporation is the publicly-traded holding company for all of the Allstate brand companies. It is not an insurer but owns all of the Allstate insurance companies of which Allstate Insurance Company is by far the largest.

Hunter (Note 2, *supra*), 24. Showing annual post-tax net income for Allstate Corporation for 2002-2006.

42   Hunter (Note 2, *supra*), 11. With chart showing the percentages for Allstate's "pure loss ratio," meaning just the amount paid for claims alone, for each year from 1987 to 2006. The percentages for 1987-2005 came from *Best's Aggregates and Averages.* The for 2006 percentage came from *Best's 2006 Allstate Company Report.*

43   Edward Liddy, CEO Allstate Corporation, presentation to Credit Suisse Insurance Conference, November 17, 2006, slide 16.

44   Hunter (Note 2, *supra*), 9-10.

45   Bold emphasis and italics in original.

46   Edward Liddy, CEO Allstate Corporation, presentation at Sanford Bernstein & Company Strategic Decisions Conference, June 6, 2006, slide 10, http://www.allstate.com/Media/ExecutiveBioSpeeches.

47   Ibid.

48   *Best's Key Rating Guide* (1999 Ed), 22. Shows Allstate's 1994 policyholder surplus to be $6,531,648,000; Allstate Corporation

2006 Annual Statement to Shareholders, 10, http://www.all-state.com/content/refresh-attachments/annual-reports/2007_ALL_anl_mtg_mtl.pdf. Shows All-state's shareholder surplus to be $21.846 billion.

49   *Best's Key Rating Guide,* (1991 Ed.), 20. This shows Allstate's 1986 policyholder surplus to be $4,081,690,000; *Best's Key Rating Guide,* (1995 Ed.), 24. Shows Allstate's 1994 policyholder surplus to be $6,531,648,000. The precise increase was $2,449,958,000, for an average yearly increase of $272,217,000.

50   *Best's Key Rating Guide,* (1991, 1994, 1998, 2002, 2007), Property/Casualty edition.

51   Allstate started building its surplus in 1931.

52   Robert Block, Allstate V.P. Investor Relations, presentation, ArgusVision 2007 conference, November 13, 2006, http://ir.allstate.com/phoenix.zhtml?c=93125&p=irol-irhome. Allstate's annual reports show that Allstate paid shareholder dividends of $3.863 billion in 2005, $2.486 billion in 2004, $1.273 billion in 2003, $675 million in 2002, $818 million in 2001, and $1.076 billion in 2000.; Allstate Corporation Annual Reports 2001-2005, page 4 in each report, http://www.allstate.com/investor/proxy/stat_statements.asp.

53   Hunter (Note 2, *supra*), 11. Graph showing Allstate paid out only 47.6¢ per premium dollar for claims in 2006.

54   Ibid., 1.

55   Ibid., 1, 10.

56   Ibid., 16.

57   Ibid., 15. "Allstate has been the leader in the property-casualty insurance industry in seeking extremely low-risk insurance underwriting. This has been harmful to consumers generally and to Allstate's policyholders in particular. As the comparative data on shareholder results provided below indicates, neither Allstate nor any property-casualty insurance company has

a business model that is financially risky. Yet *Allstate is now engaged in a major program to further reduce even this low risk, at the expense of its customers and taxpayers.*" (emphasis added). For example, these reductions include "introduction of higher two to five percent of home value deductibles and other coverage limits, such as caps on replacement costs, the exclusion or limitation of coverage for mold-related losses, the introduction of limits on payments for hail damage to roofs and the removal of automatic coverage for bringing a severely damaged home up to code" as well as exclusions for covered wind damage caused *before* flooding occurs.; Ibid., 18. The result is that Allstate has "transferred a significant amount of the risk back to policyholders."

Chapter 5: McKinsey and the "Greed is Good" Model

58 Ethan M. Rasiel, *The McKinsey Way* (McGraw-Hill 1999), xi. "Since its founding in 1923, McKinsey & Company has become the world's most successful strategic consulting firm…It may not be the largest strategy firm in the world…but it is certainly the most prestigious. McKinsey consults to most of the Fortune 100, as well as to many U.S. state and federal agencies and foreign governments. McKinsey is a brand name in international business circles." Mr. Rasiel's book is based on his personal experiences as a McKinsey associate between 1989 and 1992. Mr. Rasiel left McKinsey in 1992 just when McKinsey's project at Allstate was being proposed and accepted by Allstate's senior management. His book therefore gives some valuable insights into McKinsey's culture, methodology, and philosophy at the time McKinsey undertook the Allstate project. The Allstate project is detailed in the McKinsey slides. Many of Mr. Rasiel's observations and commentary about McKinsey and its methodology are borne out in both the style and content of the McKinsey slides which recorded McKinsey's participation in the Allstate project.

"McKinsey Over The Years," *BusinessWeek,* July 8, 2002, http://www.businessweek.com/magazine/content/02_27/b3790004.htm. Timeline for McKinsey's business.

59 *Webster's New Collegiate Dictionary* (1981 ed.), 616. The Jesuits were founded in 1534 to defend the Catholic Church against the Reformation. They have been called the "Foot Soldiers of the Pope" partly in reference to the military background of its founder, Saint Ignatius of Loyola. Although displaying high levels of skill and scholarship in their endeavors, critics have accused the Jesuits of using secrecy and intrigue to accomplish their purposes, hence the negative inference given to the term "Jesuitical" which has secondarily come to denote "one given to intrigue or equivocation."

The McKinsey Way (Note 58, *supra*), xii. "Like any strong organization, the Firm [McKinsey] has a powerful corporate culture based on shared values and common experiences. Every McKinsey-ite goes through the same rigorous training programs and suffers through the same long nights in the office. To outsiders, this can make the Firm seem monolithic and forbidding—one recent book on management consulting likened McKinsey to the Jesuits."

60 This mystique undoubtedly accounts for the numerous books written about McKinsey and its methodology.

61 *The McKinsey Way* (Note 58, *supra*), xii. "To maintain its preeminent position (and to earn its high fees) the Firm [McKinsey] seeks out the cream of each year's crop of business school graduates."

The McKinsey Way (Note 58, *supra*), 158. "McKinsey tries to skim off the cream, the elite of the elite, at the top business schools, as well as law schools and economics and finance graduate programs."

McKinsey & Company, Biography.ms., http://www.biography.ms/McKinsey_%26_Company.html, "They

[McKinsey] are the largest single recruiter at the top US business schools, including Harvard Business School, the MIT Sloan School of Management, the Wharton School, the Stanford Graduate School of Business and the Kellogg School of Management. They are also the largest recruiter at Harvard Law School and employ more Rhodes Scholars than any organization outside of the White House."

62 McKinsey & Company, Biography.ms. http://www.biography.ms/McKinsey_%26_Company.html, "More than 80 Fortune 500 CEOs are former McKinsey consultants, and McKinsey is one of the most sought after destinations for graduates of top MBA programs, having been rated #1 in the Universum survey of most desirable employers for the past six years."

63 *The McKinsey Way* (Note 58, *supra*), xi-xii, citing the achievements of McKinsey alumni Lowell Bryan (advisor to the Senate Banking Committee during the savings and loan crisis), Kenichi Ohmae (author of best seller Japanese books on management and futurology), Herb Henzler (economic and business advisor to German Chancellor Helmut Kohl), Tom Peters (management guru and coauthor of *In Search of Excellence*), Harvey Golub (president of American Express), and Adair Turner (president of Confederation of British Industries).

64 Jeffrey Skilling, Biography.ms, http://jeffrey-skilling.biography.ms/ "Skilling, born in Pittsburgh, Pennsylvania, received his B.S. in applied science at the Southern Methodist University, and his M.B.A. at Harvard Business School. He was a [partner] at McKinsey & Company before moving to Enron (around 1987), helping the company create a forward market in natural gas. He became the Chief Operating Officer in 1996, generally considered the 2nd highest position behind Ken Lay. When the latter (in February 2001) gave up his position of CEO, he designated Skilling as his replacement. Skill-

ing unexpectedly resigned on August 14 of that year, citing personal considerations, and he soon sold all of his shares in the corporation."

65 Wendy Zellner, Christopher Palmeri, Mike France, Joseph Weber, and Dan Carny, "Jeff Skilling: Enron's Missing Man," *BusinessWeek,* February 11, 2002, http://www. businessweek.com/magazine/content/02_06/b3769051.htm.

66 Alexei Barrionuevo, Kurt Eichenwald, "Skilling, on the Stand, Implies Fraud Was Hardly Necessary," *New York Times,* April 11, 2006, http://www.nytimes.com. "For all his impassioned defense of his actions, Mr. Skilling had no answer for one of the allegations against him: that he sold Enron stock in September 2001 based on insider information that the company was troubled. Mr. Skilling's stockbroker testified earlier in the trial about a taped phone call in which Mr. Skilling called in early September intending to sell 200,000 shares of Enron stock. On September 17 he increased the order to 500,000 shares."

Shaheen Pasha and Jessica Seid, "Skilling and Lay guilty of conspiracy and fraud," *CNNMoney.com,* May 25, 2006, http:// www.cnn.com/2006/BUSINESS/05/25/enron.guilty/ index.html. "Skilling was found guilty on 19 counts of conspiracy, fraud, false statements and insider trading. He was found not guilty on nine counts of insider trading."

Alexei Barrionuevo, Vikas Bajaj, and Kyle Whitmire, "The Enron Verdict: The Overview; 2 Enron Chiefs Are Convicted In Fraud And Conspiracy Trial," *New York Times,* May 26, 2006, http://www.nytimes.com. "The trial began January 30 [2006] and covered 56 days over four months."

67 *The McKinsey Way* (Note 58, *supra*), 2, "McKinsey exists to solve business problems. The consultants who succeed at McKinsey love to solve problems. As one former [McKinsey manager] put it: 'Problem solving isn't a thing you do at McKinsey; it's what you do at McKinsey. It's almost as though

you approached everything looking for ways it could be better, whatever it was. A part of you is always asking, 'Why is something done this way? Is this the best way it can be done?' You have to be fundamentally skeptical about everything.'" (emphasis in original).

Ibid., 93, "McKinsey offers [its clients] a new mindset, an outsider's view that is not locked into 'the company way' of doing things."

68 Byrne (Note 14, *supra*), "Shortly after Enron Corp. tumbled into bankruptcy last December, McKinsey & Co. Managing Partner Rajat Gupta was worried. It wasn't only because former Enron CEO Jeffrey K. Skilling was once a McKinsey & Co. partner and loyal alum. Or that his firm had advised the giant energy trader for nearly 18 years on basic strategy, even sitting in on boardroom presentations to Enron's directors. Or even that many of the underlying principles of Enron's transformation, including its 'asset-light' strategy, its 'loose-tight' culture, and the securitization of debt, were eagerly promoted by McKinsey consultants… After all, McKinsey was a key architect of the strategic thinking that made Enron a Wall Street darling. In books, articles, and essays, its partners regularly stamped their imprimatur on many of Enron's strategies and practices, helping to position the energy giant as a corporate innovator worthy of emulation."

69 Ibid.

70 As will be shown below in our discussion of McKinsey's Zero-sum Economic Game, McKinsey's CCPR system would regard policyholders as either Allstate's adversaries or else merely the victims of collateral damage in the battle to pump shareholder value by increasing net profits at any price.

71 *The McKinsey Way* (Note 58, *supra*), 17-18. "Most business problems resemble each other more than they differ. This means that with a small number of problem-solving techniques, you can answer a broad range of questions…McKin-

sey, like every other consulting firm, has developed a number of problem-solving methods and given them fancy names: Analysis of Value Added, *Business Process Redesign*, Product-Market scan, and so on. These techniques are immensely powerful. They allow McKinsey consultants very rapidly to fit the raw data that lands on their desks into a coherent framework and give them insights into the nature of the client's problem." (emphasis added).

72   Ibid., 19, noting that critics of McKinsey have said it applies the same formulas, based on the current management fads, to every problem—a "precanned answer" approach—which the author disputes as untrue.

73   Ibid., 18-19, describing a project for "a major Wall Street investment bank" seeking to reorganize IT processes and lower IT costs which the author worked on during his second year at McKinsey, 1990: "I (and the rest of the team) hardly knew where to begin. Fortunately, the Firm [McKinsey] had recently developed a new paradigm, called Business Process Redesign [BPR], that gave us a starting point. The Firm was still coming to grips with BPR, and during the study we broke new ground for the Firm. It was hard work, but BPR . . . helped us help the client force through the reorganization.".

74   C.K. Prahalad and Gary Hamel, "Core Competence Of The Corporation," *Harvard Business Review* (May-June 1990), 1-3, www.hbr.org. "Core competencies" refer to a company's collection of knowledge about how to coordinate diverse skills to achieve a strategic intent—focusing on core competencies creates a unique integrated system and competitive advantage competitors cannot copy.

75   David J. Berardinelli, *From Good Hands to Boxing Gloves: How Allstate Changed Casualty Insurance in America,* (legal edition, Trial Guides, 2006, 2008), slides 12376-12383.

76   Affidavit of Gary T. Fye, ¶ 20, *King v. Allstate Ins. Co.,* SF 97-
     3008(C), filed July 28, 1999. It seems likely McKinsey would
     have approved of USAA holding such a conference for indus-
     try insiders to discuss its USAA engagement. Such a confer-
     ence would provide a classic opportunity for McKinsey's style
     of marketing—allowing others to do the "selling" of a McKin-
     sey process. "McKinsey doesn't sell"—McKinsey "markets"
     by various forms of networking within the small and elite cir-
     cles of its potential clientele.

     Gary T. Fye is a nationally known claim handling expert in
     Reno, Nevada. Mr. Fye has consulted and testified as an expert
     in claim handling practices and procedures in a substantial
     number of cases nationwide regarding Allstate's CCPR pro-
     gram. Mr. Fye testified as one of the plaintiff's experts on
     claim handling standards during the jury trial in Utah state dis-
     trict court in the case of *Campbell v. State Farm Mut. Auto. Ins.
     Co.,* which resulted in the $149 million verdict for punitive
     damages later reversed by the United States Supreme Court.
     Campbell v. State Farm Mut. Auto. Ins. Co., 65 P.3d 1134, 1148
     (Utah 2001), describing expert testimony of Gary Fye and oth-
     ers.

     The McKinsey Way (Note 58, *supra*), 50-51 "This curious aspect
     of McKinsey's culture [McKinsey doesn't sell] stems from the
     roots of the Firm's founders in the 'white shoe' law and
     accounting firms before World War II. In those days, it was
     considered beneath the dignity of professional service firms to
     advertise or solicit business…[McKinsey gets new business]
     not because McKinsey sells, but because McKinsey *markets.*"
     (emphasis in original).

77   Affidavit of Gary T. Fye, ¶ 15, *Blanks v. Allstate Ins. Co.,* No. D-
     0101-CV-2000-00852, filed October 5, 2001.

78   "JPMorgan, TD Bank Settle Enron Claims for $480 Million,"
     Bloomberg.com, August 16, 2005, http://www.bloomberg.com/
     apps/news?pid=10000082&sid=aXlAE2sc6k.E&refer=

canada. "Enron shares lost $68 billion in value from their peak in 2000 to its December 2001 bankruptcy filing."

In addition to the extensive print and television news coverage, numerous books have been written about Enron's collapse including Kurt Eichenwald, *Conspiracy of Fools: A True Story* (Broadway Books 2005), and Bethany McLean and Peter Elkind, *The Smartest Guys in the Room: The Amazing Rise and Scandalous Fall of Enron* (Portfolio 2003) which was later made into the documentary film *Enron: The Smartest Guys in the Room* (2005). McLean and Elkind were both investigative reporters for Fortune Magazine. Strangely, McLean and Elkind seemed to completely ignore the importance of Enron and Skilling's connections to McKinsey, perhaps in deference to the wishes of Fortune's owners and editors.

79 *The Financial Services Fact Book 2006,* Chapter 5—Insurance, 70-71, http://server.iii.org/yy_obj_data/binary/669820_1_0/ Chapter5.pdf. Shows net earned premiums for the American casualty industry increasing from $294 billion in 2000 to $412.6 billion in 2004 while total financial assets reached $1.183 trillion.

"The Basics," *New York Times,* February 12, 2006, Section 4, 2. The *New York Times* ran a comparison graph attempting to give its readers some sense of scale to understand the enormity of the number 1 trillion in the context of President Bush's proposed budget of $2.77 trillion. The graph shows that a trillion is 27 times greater than the total number of acres of land on the earth (37 billion), 10 times greater than the total number of all people estimated to have ever lived (100 billion), 6.66 times greater than the total number of pennies in use (150 billion), and 2.5 times greater than the total number of stars estimated to be in the Milky Way (400 billion).

80 *The Financial Services Fact Book 2006,* Chapter 5—Insurance, http://server.iii.org/yy_obj_data/binary/669820_1_0/ Chapter5.pdf. Net casualty premiums increased $118.4 billion

in the five years between 2000 and 2004, giving an average increase of $23.68 billion per year.

81 Byrne, (Note 14, *supra*). "[O]utsiders marvel that the secretive partnership has not been drawn into the debacle, given its extensive involvement at Enron. 'I'm surprised that they haven't been subpoenaed as a witness, at least,' says Wayne E. Cooper, CEO of Kennedy Information, a research and publishing firm that keeps tabs on consultants…All of which raises uncomfortable questions about the world's most prestigious—and enigmatic—consulting firm. Did McKinsey's partners get caught up in the euphoria of the late '90s and suffer lapses of judgment? And if so, what does that say about the quality of its expensive advice? Did it stray from its core values? *What accountability does it—or any consulting firm—have for the ideas and concepts it launches into a company?*" (emphasis added).

Chapter 6: From Sears to CCPR

82 *2003 Annual Report, Amgen Inc.*, Directors and Executive Officers, 54-55, http://www.amgen.com/pdfs/Investors_2003_10k.pdf. McKinsey's marketing method is by networking. Although it may be complete coincidence, it is interesting to note that both Jerry Choate, senior Allstate executive and soon to be CEO of Allstate Corporation, and Frederick Gluck, managing partner of McKinsey from 1988-1994 were appointed to the Board of Amgen, Inc., in 1998. "Mr. Jerry D. Choate, age 65, has served as a director of the Company since August 1998. From January 1995 to January 1999, Choate served as Chairman of the Board and Chief Executive Officer of The Allstate Corporation, an insurance holding company. From August 1994 to January 1995, Choate served as President and Chief Executive Officer of Allstate and had previously held various management positions at Allstate since 1962."

83 Allstate Corporation Notice of [1999] Annual Meeting and Proxy Statement, March 26, 1999, 11-Year Summary of Selected Financial Information, C-3. This shows a total net loss for 1992 of $825 million and operating loss of $500 million.

84 "Insurance Customers Still Paying The Price," *St. Petersburg Times,* August 18, 2002, http://www.sptimes.com/2002/webspecials02/andrew/day1/story2.shtml.

85 Allstate Corporation Notice of [1999] Annual Meeting and Proxy Statement, 11-Year Summary of Selected Financial Information, C-3.

86 *C1097-5 Injury Evaluation Form,* Claim Representative Guide, 400002 (July 1, 1992). This training manual is on the Allstate CD-ROM disk available through the American Trial Lawyers Association Bad Faith Litigation Section, Volume 4, 400001-400128. "The C1097-5 was developed after considerable research and extensive field input...Any revisions to the C1097-5 must be approved by PP&C Law and Regulation and PP&C Claims in Home Office."

Ibid., 400004. Refers to the C1097-5 design work "done by the Home Office Design Team."

87 *The McKinsey Way* (Note 58, *supra*), 27. A McKinsey engagement always means significant change for a client's business systems.

88 Sears Historical Archives, http://www.searsarchives.com/history/history1980s.htm.

89 Ibid.

90 Ibid.

91 2000 Allstate Corporation Proxy Statement, SEC Schedule 14A Report, 4. "Edward M. Liddy...Chairman, President and Chief Executive Officer of Allstate from January 1995 until

1999. Before joining Allstate, Liddy was Senior Vice President and Chief Financial Officer of Sears, Roebuck and Co."

92 Ibid.

1999 Allstate Corporation Proxy Statement, 11. Lists Jerry D. Choate as Chairman and CEO of Allstate Corporation. The Allstate Corporation was incorporated on November 5, 1992, in apparent anticipation of the Sears 1993 business plan to spin off its shares of Allstate stock and turn Allstate into a publicly traded company.

1996 Allstate Annual Statement, 1996 10-K Report, 3. "The Allstate Corporation…was incorporated under the laws of Delaware on November 5, 1992 to serve as the holding company for Allstate Insurance Company…"

93 1997 Allstate Proxy Statement, 13, n. 5 "The amounts shown represents [sic] the value of the 1994, 1995 and 1996 allocations to the executive officer's account derived from employer contributions to the Profit Sharing Fund and its predecessor, The Savings and Profit Sharing Fund of Sears Employees."

94 Allstate Press Release, "Allstate CEO Establishes Stock Trading Plan," August 5, 2004, http://www.allstate.com/media/newsheadlines/pr_2004/PageRender.asp?page=pr_2004_08_05.htm. "The Allstate Corporation is the nation's largest publicly held personal lines insurer. Widely known through the 'You're In Good Hands With Allstate®' slogan, Allstate helps individuals in more than 16 million households protect what they have today and better prepare for tomorrow through more than 12,900 exclusive agencies and financial specialists in the U.S. and Canada."

95 2005 Allstate Corporation Proxy Statement, 26 (emphasis added).

96 2000 Proxy Statement for Allstate Corporation, SEC Schedule 14A Report, Notes to Consolidated Financial Statements, Nature of Operations, A-38. "Allstate's Personal Property &

Casualty ("PP&C") segment is principally engaged in private passenger auto and homeowners insurance, writing approximately 71% of Allstate's total 1999 premiums as determined under statutory accounting practices."

97   Proxy Statement for Allstate Corporation, SEC Schedule 14A Report, 1997 Board of Directors Nominees, 5. "Jerry D. Choate—Chairman of the Board and Chief Executive Officer of the company since January 1, 1995. Choate was elected President and Chief Executive Officer of the Company and a member of the Board of Directors on August 10, 1994. Previously, and since 1989, he served as Senior Executive Vice President of Allstate Insurance Company ('AIC') and as President of AIC's personal property and casualty business unit."

98   *From Good Hands to Boxing Gloves* (Note 75, *supra*), slide 4588.

99   1998 Allstate Corporation Proxy Statement, SEC Schedule 14A Report, 4, 8. Statement of total stock owned, including exercisable options; statement of options exercised, exercisable and unexercisable options, with net value of exercised and unexercised options based on $90.50 per share less the exercise price. The 1998 proxy shows Choate owned or controlled Allstate stock totaling 703,245 shares, (495,659 owned shares including 454,082 in exercisable options, plus unexercisable options on 207,596 shares—all of which would become exercisable the following year). Using the value of $90.50 per share stated in the Proxy, the total value of Choate's stock and options at the end of 1997 was $63,688,923.

100 Ibid., 13-14.

2001 Allstate Corporation Proxy Statement, SEC Schedule 14A Report, 21-23. Reciting that in addition to his stock options, which were all accelerated, and retirement plan, the Board awarded Choate an additional $3,458,000 for future "consulting" services as well as the award under Allstate's Long Term Executive Incentive Compensation Plan to which he would have been entitled had he stayed with Allstate until

2000. There is no immediate way of calculating the value of these incentive plan awards. However, by comparison, Liddy received options on approximately 400,000 shares of stock, worth about $10 million, in addition to approximately $3 million in cash bonuses under the long term incentive plan for the year 2000.

101 2005 Allstate Corporation Proxy Statement, SEC Schedule 14A Report, Table-Option Exercises in 2004 and Option Values on December 31, 2004, 19.

Ibid., Security Ownership of Directors and Executive Officers, "Insider Transaction Summary Table," Edward Liddy, 32. http://phx.corporate-ir.net/phoenix.zhtml?c=93125&p=irol-govInsiderTransDetails&id=1188983. Shows sales of 358,762 shares of Allstate stock by Liddy between August 20, 2004 and August 29, 2005, for total of $19,936,734.

2007 Allstate Corporation Proxy Statement, 36, reporting Liddy sold 646,788 shares of Allstate stock during 2006 valued at $16,471,027.

102 Ibid., 49.

103 2007 Allstate Corporation Proxy Statement, 49. Reports the value of Liddy's total retirement package at $71,763,438, including cash and vested stock options.

104 Robert Block, VP Allstate Investor Relations, ArgusVision 2007, November 13, 2006, slide 21. "Returned 74% of net income to shareholders since 1995." According to net profits from figures reported by A. M. Best from 1995, Allstate Corporation's total net income has been approximately $24 billion, 74% of which would be about $19 billion.

Chapter 7: McKinsey's Initial Presentation

105 *The McKinsey Way* (Note 58, *supra*), 3. "At McKinsey, three is a magic number. Things at the Firm come in threes...Ask a

McKinsey-ite a complex question, and you are likely to hear 'There are three reasons . . .' "

106 Ibid., 3-13. Defining the three-step process McKinsey uses to problem solve for large business organizations.

107 Ibid., 2.

108 Ibid., 9. "The essence of the initial hypothesis is 'Figure out the solution to the problem before you start.'"

109 Ibid., 8-9. Entitled "Solve The Problem At The First Meeting—The Initial Hypothesis."

110 Ibid., 72. McKinsey stores the accumulated data and business solutions obtained or created in its prior engagements in a database called "PDNet" or "Practice Development Net." PDNet is usually the first stop for any McKinsey consultant preparing for an initial IH meeting.

111 Ibid., 53-54.

112 Ibid.

113 Ibid.

The McKinsey slides don't readily reveal the names of all the McKinsey team members for the Allstate engagement. No McKinsey team names are provided in the initial presentation package. However, we know that John H. Ott was the McKinsey team "Senior Engagement Manager." McKinsey's engagement team apparently consisted of McKinsey consultants Stopher D. Bartol, M.J. Christoff, Judith Hedstrom, and Louis Marinaccio.

Carleton College, China Trip Itinerary, www.acad. carleton.edu/curricular/posc/MexChina/chinitin.html. In 2000-2003, John Ott was an office manager apparently assigned to a McKinsey office in the far east, possibly Hong Kong. On December 15, 2000, Ott hosted a delegation of students from Carleton College at a Hong Kong hotel.

Program Schedule, 3rd International Conference for Emerging Insurance Markets, http://www.oecd.org/dataoecd/44/41/2506986.pdf. On January 20, 2003, Ott was featured as a speaker employed by McKinsey at the 3rd International Conference for Emerging Insurance Markets at New Delhi, India.

114 *The McKinsey Way* (Note 58, *supra*).

115 *See The McKinsey Way* (Note 58, *supra*), 109-10. "To avoid [a] disaster scenario, McKinsey consultants engage in 'prewiring.' Before they hold a presentation or progress review, a McKinsey team will take all the relevant players in the client organization through their findings in private. That way, there are few, if any, surprises on the big day. As one former [Engagement Manager] said, 'It was very rare for us to do a presentation where we hadn't taken the various players through our findings beforehand. Otherwise, it was just too risky. In effect, the actual presentation became performance art."

116 As pointed out in *BusinessWeek* (Note 58, *supra*), McKinsey's clients pay anywhere from $10 to $60 million a year in fees. Calculating McKinsey's fees for CCPR at an average of $50 million per year for this full-time redesign project, engaging numerous teams of McKinsey consultants and lasting over eight years from 1992 through 2000, McKinsey's fees probably exceeded $250 million. To date, Allstate has avoided revealing what it paid McKinsey. Allstate has admitted that billing records exist, but has refused to produce any records showing the total fees paid to McKinsey between 1992 and 2000, claiming that McKinsey was working on "several" projects at Allstate during that time and Allstate did not "code" each project separately.

117 Combined ratios are the sum of the insurer's claim payments and all its operating expenses. Because the insurer makes investment income on every premium dollar collected, which increases the value of each premium dollar to somewhere between $1.05 to $1.15, the insurer may, as shown here, be

paying out more than the dollar it collects for claims and expenses and still make a profit. In McKinsey's initial presentation, the combined ratios quoted by McKinsey meant that in 1992 Allstate was paying out about $1.04 for claims and expenses for every premium dollar collected while State Farm was paying out about $1.03 for its claims and expenses for every premium dollar collected. Yet, because of the investment income produced while these insurers were "holding" the premiums to pay claims, both companies made an operating profit during 1992.

118 *The McKinsey Way* (Note 58, *supra*). In McKinsey-speak, "best practices" means imitation of the methods used by the "best performers" in the industry.

From Good Hands to Boxing Gloves (Note 75, *supra*), slide 10.

119 Ethan Rasiel, the author of *The McKinsey Way* states his book is based on his experiences while working at McKinsey from 1989 to 1992.

Ibid., xiv. Although Mr. Rasiel does not state when this incident occurred, he does refer to "an engagement for a major insurance company" in which the McKinsey team's initial hypothesis was that the insurer could regain its profitability by "eliminating 'leakage'—the acceptance of customer claims without adjustment."

Ibid., 21. Whether this was a reference to McKinsey's pre-1992 State Farm engagement is unknown. However, the term "leakage" appears numerous times in McKinsey's initial presentation to Allstate.

120 *From Good Hands to Boxing Gloves* (Note 75, *supra*), slide 13 (bold emphasis in original).

121 *Strengthening the Surveillance System—Final Report*, McKinsey & Company, National Association of Insurance Commissioners (April 1974), available in hard copy from the NAIC. This doc-

ument outlines procedures for regulatory examination of insurers to check for misconduct in handling claims.

122 *From Good Hands to Boxing Gloves* (Note 75, *supra*), slide 5166.

123 Ibid., slide 2930.

124 Ibid., slide 14. Paragraphs 5-6 omitted because of a gap in the author's notes (emphasis added).

Chapter 8: The Zero-sum Game

125 *From Good Hands to Boxing Gloves* (Note 75, *supra*), slide 5166.

126 Leslie Eaton and Joseph Treater, "Patchwork City—Insurers Bear Brunt Of Anger In New Orleans," *New York Times,* September 3, 2004.

127 *From Good Hands to Boxing Gloves* (Note 75, *supra*), 1426, 9722.

128 *Egan v. Mutual of Omaha Insurance Co.,* 620 P.2d 141, 146 (Cal.1979) (citations omitted) (emphasis added).

129 *From Good Hands to Boxing Gloves* (Note 75, *supra*), slide 2929 (emphasis added).

130 *Wikipedia, Liebeck v. McDonald's Restaurants,* http://en. wikipedia.org/wiki/McDonald's_coffee_case#cite_ref-7 (accessed April 2008).

131 Ibid.

132 "I'm Being Sued for WHAT?", *ABC News Special Report,* May 2, 2007, http://abcnews.go.com/TheLaw/Story?id= 3121086&page=1 (accessed April 2008).

133 Ibid.

134 *National Underwriter Property & Casualty Magazine,* "P-C Insurers' Income Soars to $64B In 2006," posted April 18, 2007, http://prop ertyandcasualtyinsurancenews.com/cms/ NUPC/Breaking %20 News/2007/04/18-ISOPCI2006-- ss?searchfor=combined%20ratio (accessed April 2008).

135 *National Underwriter Property & Casualty Magazine,* April 23, 2007, at 6-7 (hereafter referenced as *National Underwriter*).

136 *Wikipedia,* "Insurance Services Office," http://en.wikipedia.org/wiki/Insurance_Services_Office (access April, 2008). Insurance Services Office, Inc., "ISO," is a provider of data, underwriting, risk management and legal/regulatory services to property-casualty insurers and other clients. Headquartered in Jersey City, New Jersey, the organization serves clients with offices throughout the United States, along with international operations offices in the United Kingdom, Israel, Germany, India and China. ISO is made of hundreds of "member" insurance companies who rely on its data and regulatory filings regarding premium rates and policy forms. ISO has developed enormous databases of information about hundreds of millions of individual insurance policies, along with a large volume of public records pertaining to fraud, real property, employment screening, and motor vehicles. ISO also monitors regulatory standards and insurance laws, and makes many filings and other communications with regulatory authorities on behalf of its clients.

Deposition of Richard Biondi, *King v. Providence Washington Ins. Co.,* SF 91-141(C), Santa Fe County, New Mexico, April 11, 1995, at 39-46.

137 Harvey W. Rubin, *Dictionary Of Insurance Terms,* 277 (Barron's 3rd ed. 1995)."Reserves" or "loss reserves" are the amount of money a casualty insurer must designate from earned premiums for claims it knows have been incurred or are due but which have not yet been paid.

National Underwriter, 6.

138 *Wikipedia,* http://en.wikipedia.org/wiki/McDonald's _coffee_case#cite_ref-7 (accessed April 2008). Wikipedia reports that in late 2005, billboards were put up around San Francisco stating "Spill hot coffee on your lap, win millions! Play Lawsuit Lotto!"

Chapter 9: Good Hands or Boxing Gloves

139 Ibid., slide 3372 (emphasis added).

140 Ibid., slide 10096, 10098.

Deposition of Toni M. Boyd (Note 8, *supra*).

141 Ibid., slide 12504.

142 *The Living Webster Encyclopedic Dictionary of the English Language,* (1977 ed.), 779. "A victory, as that gained by King Pyrrhus of Epirus [Greece] over the Romans in 279 B.C., costing more to the victor than to the vanquished."

143 Deposition of Allstate Adjuster Susan Cary, *Armijo v. Allstate Indem. Co.,* D-0101-CV-2002-0318, at 188-89 "Q. [I]t is true, is it not, that *CCPR protocols are exactly the same* in the represented cases involving UM [uninsured motorist] claims as in the represented cases involving third-party claims? A. Yes." (emphasis added).

144 *From Good Hands to Boxing Gloves* (Note 75, *supra*), slide 6325.

145 Ibid. Whether these quotes are real or apocryphal is probably beside the point McKinsey was trying to make (emphasis added).

146 Anderson, Gordon and Liben, "Insurance Nullification By Litigation," *Risk Management Magazine,* 46-50 (April, 1994) (emphasis added).

147 Ibid.

148 *Campbell v. State Farm Mut. Auto. Ins. Co.,* 98 P.3d 409, 415 (Utah 2004), *cert. denied,* 125 S.Ct. 114 (2004) (quote marks and citations omitted) (emphasis added).

149 *Hayseeds, Inc. v. State Farm Fire & Cas.,* 352 S.E.2d 73, 79 (W.Va.1986). "We adopted this rule in recognition of the fact that, when an insured purchases a contract of insurance, he

buys insurance—not a lot of vexatious, time-consuming, expensive litigation with his insurer."

Chapter 10: We Get What We Measure

150 *From Good Hands to Boxing Gloves* (Note 75, *supra*), slide 2930.

151 Ibid., slide 3020.

152 *Martinez, et al. v. Allstate Ins. Co., et al.,* D-0101-CV-2004-0963. Affidavit of Shannon Kmatz, April 13, 2003 [Human Resources], Affidavit of Shannon Kmatz, April 13, 2003 [Big Blue].

153 Ibid.

154 *From Good Hands to Boxing Gloves* (Note 75, *supra*), slide 10685.

155 PDS Report of Susan Cary, March 1997, produced in *Blanks v. Allstate Ins. Co.,* D-0101-CV-2000-0852. In Allstate employee PDS reports generated from 1995-97, the "Paid to EA" or "% to EA" was stated for each adjuster in terms of past performance and future goals. In apparent response to New Mexico state courts ordering Allstate to produce these PDS reports without confidentiality restriction, and their subsequent dissemination to other bad faith plaintiffs across the country, Allstate stopped using the "% to EA" figures. This same measurement was instead covertly included under a general performance goal entitled "adherence to process."

156 Harvey W. Rubin, *Dictionary of Insurance Terms*, 247 (Barron's 3rd Ed. 1995). One of the expenses which form part of the premium dollar calculation is "Loss Adjustment Expense" or "LAE". As the name implies, this also includes the salaries of the insurer's claims employees.

157 The exception is the situation where the policyholder is required by law to buy the insurance for the protection of others, such as mandatory car liability insurance. Here, some courts correctly recognize that such policies are intended by

law to benefit the third party or the public in general and so certain traditional rules also apply to the treatment of these claimants as well. *Hovet v. Allstate Ins. Co.,* 2004-NMSC-10, 135 N.M. 397, 89, P.3d 69.

158 *Zilisch v. State Farm Mutual Auto Ins. Co.,* 995 P.2d 276, 280 (Ariz. 2000).

159 Lt. Col. Karl E. Wingenbach, "Kill Box—The Newest FSCM," 1-2, http://sill-www.army.mil/FAMAG/2005/JUL_AUG_2005/PAGES13_15.pdf. A military tactical term indicating a coordinated plan of attack for air and ground forces in which all enemy targets within a designated geographic area are systematically attacked and destroyed.

Dan's History, "Military Aviation Terms and Definitions," http://www.danshistory.com/glossary.shtml. "A designated area of terrain that is routinely patrolled by strike/attack aircraft. Any targets found within the 'box' are subject to immediate lethal attack and destruction."

Chapter 11: Stepping Into the Ring

160 Ibid., 600109. "Recommended Attorney Performance Measures ... Measure ... Results: Performance vs. evaluated amount: Percent of cases closed at or below evaluated amount ... aggregate dollar and percentage deviation from evaluated amount ... Consistency: Actual resolution method vs. initial resolution method ..."

Ibid., 600117. "Comparison Of Current And Proposed Approaches For Managing Retained Counsel ... Optimal Approach: Reward for results on an aggregate of cases handled ...".

161 Ibid., 600246-248. Staff counsel compensation will be "linked" to performance measure—number of cases tried or settled at or below the "evaluated amount."

162 Ibid., 600341.

163 *Allstate CCPR Litigation Management Manual,* 600075, summary of litigation plans.

Ibid., at 600132, summary of litigation plans.

164 *Givens v. Allstate Insurance Company, et al.,* 75 S.W.3d 383, at 391-94 (Tenn. 2002).

165 Domestic Abuse Insurance Protection Act., NMSA 1978, § 59A-16B-6 (1997).

Insurance Trade Practices and Frauds Act, NMSA 1978, § 59A-16-20(O) (1997).

166 *Guest v. McLean, et al.,* No. 26,813, New Mexico Court of Appeals (filed February 29, 2008), at ¶¶ 2, 14, 16, and *Guest v. Berardinelli and McLean,* No. 26,813, New Mexico Court of Appeals. In this case, Allstate's lawyer sued me personally, and another lawyer representing the Allstate policyholders, for including her in the policyholders' bad faith lawsuit against Allstate for using the CCPR tactics described in the opinion. Her case was dismissed by the district court and this opinion affirms that dismissal. On April 4, 2008, the Allstate lawyer filed a motion for reconsideration with the Court of Appeals. That motion was denied on April 8, 2008.

167 *Allstate Insurance Company v. Fields,* No. 45A03-0612-CV-602, Indiana Court of Appeals (filed November 9, 2007).

168 *Holladay v. Allstate Ins. Co.,* No. D-0101-CV-2001-00103. In that case, the policyholder was a plumber with a small business who had recently moved to New Mexico from California. He was unaware at the time that New Mexico, unlike California, requires businesses to charge sales tax for professional services. The case was settled before we could question the New Mexico tax authorities about who had provided the "tip" about the policyholder's failure to pay proper sales taxes. However, the only people who had the policyholder's financial information at the time of the "tip" were the policyholder, his bookkeeper, and the Allstate claims supervisor. Both the poli-

cyholder and the bookkeeper denied being the "tipster," leaving the Allstate claims supervisor as the only logical suspect.

Chapter 12: Colossus

169 The name *Colossus* is well known in the computer industry. It was the name of the first programmable computer built in 1943 by the British in Bletchley Park, England, to decode the German military codes. Colossus was also the name of a famous fictional supercomputer with artificial intelligence in the 1969 cult movie classic *Colossus: The Forbin Project*. In a plot line similar to the later *Terminator* films, Colossus takes over the United States nuclear arsenal and then threatens to wipe out the human population by a global nuclear conflagration with the warning to humans: "Obey me and live. Disobey me and die."

170 Aaron DeShaw, D.C., J.D., *Colossus: What Every Trial Lawyer Needs To Know* (Trial Guides, 2004). An excellent discussion of the history, workings, and weaknesses of Colossus, hereafter referenced as "DeShaw."

James Mathis, *How Colossus Works*, http://www.sequoiavisions.com. Another valuable reference on this topic.

171 P. Beinat and E. Tsui, "Extending Colossus To Cover Compensation For Future Economic Loss," *Intelligent Systems in Accounting, Finance and Management Journal* 1 (1992), 275-287.

172 Ibid.

173 Ibid.

174 Ibid.

175 Harvey W. Rubin, *Dictionary Of Insurance Terms* (3rd ed. 1995), 73.

176 Ibid., 120. The best example of a defined benefit policy is the "death and dismemberment" coverage sometimes attached to auto policies, which pay a definite sum for loss of a hand, arm,

leg, eye, etc. These benefits are paid regardless of the actual loss resulting from the injury.

177 DeShaw, 56-57 (quoting Beinat & Tsui, Note 171, *supra*).

178 Ibid.

179 Ibid.

180 Declaration of Robert Dietz, *Farmers Ins. Ex. v. Dietz, et al.,* 02-2-10109-5 (Snohomish County, Washington).

Robert Dietz, "The Rise of Colossus," continuing legal education presentation, Washington Trial Lawyers conference, November 22, 2002.

Deposition of Robert Dietz, *Armijo v. Allstate Indem. Co.,* D-0101-CV-2002-0318. Hereafter referenced collectively as "Dietz."

181 DeShaw (Note 170, *supra*), 24-25.

182 Dietz (Note 180, *supra*). The information in this chapter until Note 183 is drawn from Dietz.

183 *Truong et al. v. Allstate Ins. Co., et al.,* CV 99-003474, Response to Plaintiff's Motion to Supplement Record.

184 *State of Louisiana v. Allstate Insurance Company, et al.,* 07-14595, Parish of Orleans, filed October 8, 2007. "In truth, however, these insurers, (together with ISO, McKinsey, Xactware, and MSB), through Xactimate and/or IntegriClaim, intentionally devalue the 'market price' in order to underpay their policyholders and/or artificially deflate construction and repair costs in the affected market."

185 One company which used Colossus, Farmers, has agreed to stop its use of Colossus for policyholder claims, as part of the settlement of a class action brought in Oklahoma.

Chapter 13: Allstate on the Gulf Coast

186 *Weiss v. Allstate Ins. Co.,* ED Louisiana, 06-CV-3774.

187 Ibid.

188 "Allstate Unit Pricing Challenged After Katrina," *New Orleans Times Picayune,* May, 20, 2007 (emphasis added).

189 *Weiss v. Allstate,* No. 06-3774

190 Brian Faler, "Lott 'Scorned' After Katrina, Targets State Farm, Allstate," *Bloomberg.com,* May 20, 2007, http://www. bloomberg.com/apps/news?pid=20601070&sid=aYjjlGy PeitA

Chapter 14: Redefining the Game

191 National Center for State Courts.

192 *State Farm v. Campbell,* 538 U.S. 408, 123 S.Ct. 1513, 155 L.Ed.2d 585 (2003).

193 *Williams v. Philip Morris Inc.,* 540 US 801, 124 S Ct 56, 157 L Ed 2d 12 (2003).

194 Hunter, 19.

195 Ibid.

Epilogue

196 *Fields, et al. v. Allstate Insurance Company, et al.,* No. 45C01-9510-CT-11927, Lake County Circuit Court, Indiana.

197 *Deer, et al. v. Allstate Insurance Company, et al.,* No. 0516-CV24031, Jackson County Circuit Court, Missouri.

198 http://www.floir.com/pressreleases/viewmediarelease. aspx?id=2858 (accessed January 2008).

199 *Fojas v. Allstate Corporation, et al.*, No. 80-CV-423, U.S. District Court, Northern District of Illinois.

200 Ibid., ¶ 27.